S0-AXX-962

Dating
NO GUTS, NO GLORY

Dear Cindy,

We hope you enjoy this fun book. And its loving message. Remember how much your Father in Heaven loves you. We love you too.

Young Women's Presidency.

Sept, 02

OTHER COVENANT BOOKS BY JONI HILTON

As the Ward Turns, a novel

Around the Ward in 80 Days, a novel

Scrambled Home Evenings, a novel

Guilt-Free Motherhood

Honey on Hot Bread & Other Heartfelt Wishes

That's What Friends Are For, a novel

Dating
NO GUTS, NO GLORY

a novel

JONI HILTON

Covenant Communications, Inc.

Listen. Any similarities between your name and the name of somebody in this book is not only an incredible coincidence, but possibly even quite ironic. I therefore recommend that you buy a dozen copies or so, if for no other reason than to hand them out and say, "Look at this—can you believe it?"

Cover images ® 2000 PhotoDisc, Inc.

Cover design copyrighted 2000 by Covenant Communications, Inc.

Published by Covenant Communications, Inc.
American Fork, Utah

Printed in the United States of America
First Printing: July 1989

07 06 05 04 03 02 01 00   10 9 8 7 6 5 4 3 2 1

ISBN 1-57734-610-6

For my husband, Bob, the world's greatest date . . . who still makes me fall down laughing one minute, then cry with spiritual wonder the next . . . who's the perfect father and yet my exciting hero into whose arms I gladly melt.

And for our children, Richie, Brandon, and Cassidy. May their dating years lead them to spouses as gutsy and glorious as mine.

CHAPTER ONE

Grand Night

Get this: Marky Davis, who built an international reputation for himself among babysitters as the most obnoxious, shameless brat ever to fire a spitwad, is now president of the Fremont High School senior class.

This was a kid whose very name made people roll their eyes and shake their heads. When his parents would drag him into church (the only way you could ever get Marky to go anywhere), people would sit at least ten feet away, leaving an empty radius all around Marky's family. To venture closer would pose risk to life and limb, as Marky was the only kid in his ward ever known to hurl a Lego into the overhead lights. Heaven only knew what could happen to you if you got too close to Marky just as his mom was popping the lid to his Tupperware cache of Cheerios.

I know all this—and more—not because I was one of the horrified Mia Maid babysitters (with Cheerios tossed down my blouse and into my bra), but because one of my big brothers, Bill, is engaged to marry one such former Mia Maid. Her name is Wendy (can you believe Bill actually lets this woman call him Sugarbill?) and she gave me the whole scoop on Marky. Her family lives in Marky's ward, in our same stake.

While Marky, who is my age, was rolling with the speed of a champion bowling ball under the chapel benches, knocking into old women's calves and canes, I was sitting obediently beside my parents in another ward, thoughtfully analyzing the sacrament meeting speaker and keeping my little white-gloved hands folded daintily in my lap. Okay, so maybe that's not *exactly* what I was doing, but you can be dead certain I wasn't running up and down the aisles, my shirttail flapping, my shoes untied, and using a baby bottle filled with grape juice as a squirt gun.

It isn't all hearsay. I've bumped into him once or twice, too, even though we attend different schools. Once, since we're in the same stake, I saw him at a youth conference. He was wearing a pink muumuu, wiggling his hips and strumming a ukulele in a Hawaiian show that his ward provided as the "entertainment." Not only was he not even slightly embarrassed (which he should have been), he was in his glory, laughing his head off.

The other time, I saw him coming out of a movie theater at the mall, wearing an upside-down popcorn box as a hat.

So it was with no small amount of shock and amazement that I discovered Mark Davis (still Marky under that cool exterior) had been voted class president of Fremont, the rival to my own Whitney High School, in what had to be one of the shadiest elections in the history of high-school politics.

All these thoughts tumbled through my now-educated little mind, as I sat sweltering in the heat of Fremont High's graduation. James Olbern, a good friend from my ward, goes to Fremont and asked me to attend his graduation and then go with him to Grad Night. Ward boundaries in California are sometimes so big that you can have five or six schools represented in one ward. James, for example, lives two blocks from me, and right between us is the border between Fremont and Whitney. (Whitney, of course, being the superior school. Hey, it's my book and I can write what I want. If James wants equal time for Fremont, let him write his own book.)

Whitney High's graduation had been last week, so I sat there feeling very adult in the bleachers with people who were mostly parents, worlds away from high school days. I wonder if any of them were as shocked as I was, when I sat down and opened the graduation program and saw Mark Davis listed as senior class president. What was his campaign platform—skateboarding in the hallways?

I looked down onto the football field. The heftiest of the P.E. teachers had set up the folding chairs, and now the senior class—looking like an assemblage of Martians in their green caps and gowns—sat on the football field, waiting for Principal Sternbach to finish his preposterous talk onto which he had slapped the dubious title "I Have Seen the Future, and It Is the Fremont High School Graduating Class."

He had sweat running down his ruddy neck, and he didn't even have to wear one of those green Martian suits. (Speaking of Fremont's school colors, I'll bet they'd like to get their hands on the prankster who picked hospital green for a school whose mascot is a Freedom Fighter. You'd think red, white, and blue, maybe. At least blue. Instead, here they are dressed like a bunch of amateur surgeons suiting up for the kind of surgery that keeps malpractice lawyers in business.)

I looked around at the sea of surgeons. Squinting, I found a few more kids I knew. There was Alvin Eisenstat, the last guy—next to Marky Davis—who I'd trust with a scalpel. I pictured him walking through hospital halls and being paged, "Dr. Eisenstat. Stat." Yeah, Eisenstat-stat. Alvin, the champion burper who can sing the entire "Star Spangled Banner" in one solid belch, would push his glasses up onto his greasy nose, and probably head in the wrong direction. I imagined him in surgery, dressed in that queasy green, carving into some poor victim and belching, "Oops."

I looked across the aisle from Alvin. There was Merissa Purley, her eyes actually tear-filled as she listened to Principal Sternbach. Merissa, give me a break. Sternbach probably gives the same speech every year, just like our principal does at Whitney. Well, maybe she didn't know that. Maybe she needs to read a few back issues of the *Fremont Free Press.* It's undoubtedly in there every year.

Somebody was popping their gum behind me, and a dog was lying on the grass off to the left, eating a paper cup. A fly buzzed among the crowd, getting waved away from row to row. We bleacher-bound observers sat fanning ourselves with graduation programs that misspelled every tenth name. We looked like a group of shipwrecked travelers, signaling with white cards for passing aircraft to rescue us.

Finally Sternbach sat down. Now it was time to hear from the school valedictorian, whom the powers that be had decided to keep secret this year. I figured it would probably be Merissa Purley or maybe Jeff Lincoln, the computer whiz kid. This was a brainy guy if ever there was one—he not only won the state science fair when he was in the tenth grade, he went on to design and run the next two school science fairs for Fremont. I remember reading about him in the paper. The man is a genius, what can I say? (Not smart enough, however, to ask me on a date despite my continual hinting through some girls I know at Fremont. Oh, well. I've always found brilliance extremely attractive. There's just one problem: brilliance does not always reciprocate.)

Then the vice principal introduced the valedictorian. My jaw nearly hit my lap. It was Mark Davis. Mark stepped up to the podium and actually blushed. Oh, please, I thought. Not only did he somehow finagle his way into being the valedictorian, but now he's actually trying to feign humility. This was simply too much. I sat staring, my mouth still open wide enough to entice cave spelunkers.

"Hey, Louisa," I heard someone whisper. I looked down my row a few seats to Travis Bailey, a guy from Whitney who, like me, was here because his date for tonight was a girl graduating from Fremont. (Imagine graduating from high school and then immediately having to go on a date with Travis Bailey—it's a wonder she didn't fail a few tests and get held back on purpose.) In fact, several kids from Whitney were here waiting for their dates.

Travis was leaning forward, his elbows on his knees, and he was craning sideways to get my eye. "Louisa Barker!" he hissed. "You drooling over Mark Davis?"

I nearly gagged. "Oh. Right," I said, trying to sound as sarcastic as possible. Then Travis mimicked me, staring at Mark with his mouth hanging open as if he were swooning. I watched Travis run out his rope on this little scenario and just shook my head. I'm so glad I'm out of high school, I thought. Away from half-wits like Travis Bailey and out of a system that rewards a scoundrel like Mark Davis by making him valedictorian.

I listened to Mark's speech, which I couldn't believe was interrupted by applause four separate times. Why not just run for office, Mark? He was so glib, so funny, it just made me madder. And then he worked in a little gospel doctrine, which would have pleased me immensely had anyone else been giving that speech. (Me, for example.)

"I wonder who wrote that speech for him," I found myself muttering. Jill Barnes, another student from Whitney, who manages to talk down to everybody she knows, including those who are a jump or two ahead of her (and this would define just about everyone), patted me on the shoulder. Have you ever patted somebody on the shoulder who was already sitting smack next to you? That gesture was a feat of engineering that ought to have earned Jill a scholarship to Cal Poly.

Anyway, she patted me in that wiser-than-thou way usually reserved for Great Aunts and said, "I happen to know he's a straight-A student, Louisa."

"Yeah, well, your secret is safe with me," I whispered. Then I glanced down at Travis Bailey again. He was still mugging and pulling faces. Travis, like too many other guys in high school, is about eighty-five percent hormones and fifteen percent hair.

"See Travis Bailey?" I nudged Jill. She looked down at Travis, who was now wagging his tongue like a pendulum and rolling his eyes in opposite rhythm. This was his Kit Cat impersonation—you know, the plastic cat clocks with rhinestones on them that glance back and forth as the clock ticks? I saw Travis do this bit at a party once. I made note of who thought it was funny and decided never to buy jokes from those same people, should I ever grow up and become a comedienne.

Anyway, Jill's face registered the appropriate level of disgust, and I took the opportunity to say, "Can you believe Travis is going to Harvard on a full scholarship?"

Jill spun around and stared incredulously at me. "No—really?"

"It's the truth," I lied. "And you know the math teacher, Miss Billingsly? She just signed a contract with RCA—she's cutting a country western album. And you know Coach Hoxie? He's gonna be the lead guitarist."

Now Jill, who has never been accused of being a terrific sport, just glared at me and turned her attention back to Mark the Magnificent.

By now Mark was wrapping up his speech. He'd said some pretty good things about making opportunities rather than waiting for them to come to you, I decided that this had probably been his motto from childhood, having taken the opportunity to do every conceivable daring deed that a toddler could do. So maybe he did write his speech. But straight-A's? Not even Mark could pull *that* one off.

In a few minutes, James and his class all had their blank diplomas (the real ones were to be mailed a few weeks later), and kids were tossing their green hats into the air, shedding their green gowns, and gearing up for Grad Night. Traditionally, Fremont High went to Disneyland for this all-night event, along with several other schools, including Whitney.

We piled into a bus that was probably made in the same factory that turns out those shopping carts with the wheels that lock in four different directions—you know those carts? Why isn't it yet an Olympic event to steer one of those through the aisles of a supermarket? You want a good research project to do for extra credit someday? Find out the percentage of asylum residents who can trace their troubles to shopping carts with jammed wheels—it's gotta be at least sixty per cent.

Anyway, the driver got lost four different times. Now, pretend you're on a game show. What famous amusement park is the best-labeled in the world and has the most freeway signs directing tourists to it? If you answered Disneyland, congratulations! You're right! You win a free trip to the Bus Drivers Academy of Anaheim, California.

We finally got there, just in time to see the line to every good ride reach its maximum, record-breaking length. But James Olbern is a good sport and we lined up with lots of other kids we knew so the time in line seemed to go pretty fast.

My two best friends, Heather and Kelly, were there with their dates, trying to talk the guys into going into the Tiki Room. This is a Polynesian-themed non-ride sponsored by Dole, where it seems like you spend the first ten minutes staring at a dribbly little fountain of colored water that splashes down over a plastic pineapple. Then you're treated to the animation wizardry of four chattery, stuffed parrots, and flowers whose petals clack as they sing. I sided with the guys, but didn't say anything.

Of course everybody wanted to go on Star Tours, Space Mountain, and Pirates of the Caribbean. James and I thought we'd head over to the Haunted Mansion and maybe grab something to eat in New Orleans Square.

On the way, we met up with some more friends and they talked us into going on the Mad Tea Party teacups. Have you been on those?

You sit in giant, spinning teacups that whirl so fast you can hardly sit up straight. Everything in the background becomes a blur, and all you can hear is goofy Alice in Wonderland music with pops, bangs, and whistles in it. Everybody loves it.

While James and I were waiting for our turn, two other huge crowds of kids joined the line. Then just as the gate opened for us to find teacups, a crush of teenage humanity poured in with us, twirling us around and separating us in the stampede. I looked all over for James and couldn't find him. Suddenly somebody grabbed my hand and pulled me into a teacup. The little door closed and the teacup started twirling.

I looked up, thinking James had somehow found me in the swarm of confusion, and instead stared straight into the face of Mark Davis.

I'd like to tell you that I reacted calmly and said (to paraphrase Higgins' prim and proper mother in *My Fair Lady)*, "Why Mark Davis, what a disagreeable surprise." Or better yet, that I smiled politely and considered it an honor to be trapped in a teacup with Fremont's valedictorian. But I wasn't exactly as gracious at that.

I screamed.

"It's okay, I'm here," he said. Oh, *this is just great!* He thinks I'm scared because I'm all by myself. Or because there are so many pushing, shouting kids all around us.

I gasped for a new breath to clarify my dismay, but it was too late. The ride had started and Mark was cranking the center wheel for all he was worth. Our teacup was nearly airborne. When I stole a glance at the other teacups, the 0-forces whipped my head around, where it stuck in Far Right gear. Nobody was spinning as fast as we were. Nobody.

In fact, I suspect that in the history of Disneyland, no one has spun as fast as we did. Why that spinner disk didn't snap off in Mark's frenzied hands is a mystery to me.

Using all the strength my neck muscles could muster, I managed to turn my head again and look at Mark. Surely my terrified expression would slow him down.

Not a chance. He saw my face and only grinned more.

"We've really got her going, huh?"

What's this "we" stuff, Mark? I thought. You got a mouse in your pocket? Then again, the way we were spinning, Mark probably had a gorilla in his pocket.

Over Mark's shoulder I could see some more teacups zooming by, and rising from the rim of one cup, like a groundhog coming up out of his hole, was Travis Bailey.

"Hey—there's Louisa with Mark Davis! Oooh, Louisa, what happened to James?"

Never have I so wished for someone to spin fast enough that he'd go flying out of his teacup and land on his ear. Of all times to be with Mark Davis—just as Travis Bailey goes whizzing by. Now nothing would ever convince him that I didn't have a crush on Mark. I closed my eyes. Who cared what Travis thought, anyway?

Mark was crouching over the steering wheel now, really getting into it.

Suddenly I remembered a film I saw in a health class once. It showed how they use blood that you donate. These guys in lab coats clamp little test tubes of blood into a big barrel that spins like crazy until they've separated out the plasma or the corpuscles or whatever it is they need besides regular red blood. This is what was happening to me right now. I could feel it in my veins. I may as well just stagger off the ride and donate my entire body to science. The whole thing is all divided up for them and ready.

The wacky mad-hatter music was spinning through me like a synthesizer gone berserk, the sound effects seeming to hammer into my head with a ten-pound mallet. Suddenly I found the way to keep kids from ever trying drugs. You take them to Disneyland and you make them ride the teacup ride with Mark Davis. Just before they throw up, you tell them that this is what drugs do to your brain. I guarantee those kids will stay off drugs forever.

Finally, as if angels had descended and taken over the ride controls, the teacups began to wind down. (Ours wound down last, of course.) My pupils were pounding with my heart: big-small, big-small, big-small.

Mark leaped out of the teacup, then reached back to pull me, limp and dizzy, from the jaws of death. (This is another good reason why tea is against the Word of Wisdom, I'll bet.)

Everything seemed tilted, even Mark's laughing smile, as he tried to steady me toward the exit. "C'mon, Louisa," he said. "Just ten more feet."

I felt like all ten of those feet were attached to my ankles, and each one wanted to go in a different direction. Great Scott—I've become a shopping cart! This was more bizarre than anything that *ever* happened to Alice in Wonderland.

At the exit, James was standing there with his arms folded. Mark deposited me in the arms of my date, who led me to a bench where I promptly collapsed.

When the world finally steadied itself again, I asked James what had happened. Evidently so many kids had stormed the gate that James had been left without a teacup, and had had to exit. It was not, he reported, the highlight of his life to watch his date go spinning in a turquoise teacup with the president of his senior class.

I tried to explain that I'd virtually been kidnapped, and then tortured in a blood centrifuge, but James had worked up a good pout and was not about to abandon his wounded warrior pose. Finally I said, "Okay, you name the ride. What can I go on to make it up to you?"

James just looked at me and grinned. "The teacups," he said.

I gulped. "Fine. I'm more than willing to be sacrificed on the altar of the Mad Hatter so that you will believe I did not plan a secret rendezvous with Mad Mark Davis. No problem."

James gave me a hug. "Forget it. Let's just go to the Haunted Mansion."

We stood up and I was relieved to note that the nerves from my brain to my legs were working almost at full capacity again, and my feet were in fact following commands to walk.

First, we headed for the air-conditioned theater of the Country Bear Jamboree so I could catch my breath, then past the western storefronts of Frontierland. Just as I was truly beginning to de-program from the brain-wash, brain-spin, brain-dry of the teacups, there was Mark Davis again. Only this time a bunch of guys were carrying him over their heads like he'd just won the Superbowl. Mark was now wearing Mickey Mouse ears, and looking for all the world like the hero in a Disney movie about lovable little rodents, who are rodents nonetheless.

"Fre-mont wins! Fre-mont wins!" the guys were shouting. Just then Chas Robinson, a popular guy from Whitney and the very embodiment of cool, athletic prowess, walked up. "Man, did you see that?" he said. "We had a contest at the shooting gallery, me and this guy from Fremont. That guy never missed!"

"Mark Davis?" James asked.

"Yeah, I think that was his name. Man, I thought I had him, too. I only missed three."

"Well, well," I whispered to James. "Looks like Mark Davis is just scattering joy all over the Magic Kingdom." Then I turned to Chas. "Oh, forget it, Chas," I said. "Those things are rigged anyway."

Chas pretended to be personally offended. "Not at *Disneyland,*" he said, surprised that I would suggest such a thing. "Louisa, bite your tongue. What would Walt say?"

"Walt would say, 'Take those ears off Mark Davis and force him to ride the teacups for twenty hours straight.'"

Chas laughed. "You're a good sport, Chas," James said.

"Hey, man, I'm just cool." Then Chas slapped palms with a buddy of his who had just walked up, and they shook hands in some complicated ritual they both knew. Already, Chas had forgotten the shooting gallery and was probably off to the Matterhorn. James and I headed on.

"Looks like Mark Davis rides again," James said, looking sideways at me to measure how much this annoyed me. No matter how irritating it is to be teased about liking someone you don't, you have to quietly endure it or, for some unexplainable reason, it will prove that your accuser is right, and that you are hopelessly in love with the guy. The more loudly you protest, the more others are convinced that they've uncovered the romance of the century.

I rolled my eyes. "C'mon," I said and linked my arm through James's. "Let's go ride those crazy teacups together."

CHAPTER TWO
The Dating Panel

I decided to stay home for the summer before heading off to BYU. Since I'm the youngest kid in the family—in fact the only person you could still call "a kid"—my parents wanted to postpone having an empty nest. And, to be honest, I knew that going off to college was a big step toward adulthood, a step I'd just as soon delay. This could be my last summer to be a barefoot teenager with both the freezer and refrigerator doors open as I look for something to eat, while I'm talking on the phone and pulling on the phone cord with my toes (all things that bug my mom, but that I'm pretty sure she'll miss once I'm gone).

I knew this could be my last summer to enjoy a bedroom full of high school memorabilia, stuffed animals on my pillows, and shades of pink that I'll probably never see again until *I* have daughters. I'm not saying that I think I'll be married before coming home again. I might not marry for years. But once I go away to school and start paying my own bills, repairing my own sinks, running my own schedule, and answering to my own newly responsible self, I have a feeling I'll see this old bedroom differently—it will look like a child's room, or the room of a girl who's suddenly much younger than I am.

Okay, I also decided to stay home so I could bankroll a few bucks to see me through Mall Days at BYU. Mall Days is not an official holiday, of course, but my own invention, since I suspect that I will create several such excuses to shop for stuff I'm sure I'll need once I get there. Clothes come to mind.

So to finance this plan, I got a job working—where else?—in a bookstore at the local mall. I've always liked books and I used to volunteer in grade school as a library helper (largely so I could read all the new books before a bunch of kids got cookie crumbs in the creases). Also, it got me out of tumbling class (today they call it gymnastics, but if *I'm* doing it—believe me—it's still tumbling).

When I interviewed for the job, the manager asked me what books I had recently read. Yikes! I'd been so busy studying for finals that I hadn't done any reading for fun in quite a while. I thought and finally mumbled, "I, uh . . . I've only had time for my scripture reading lately." I told him about how I had the toughest teachers ever invented by the Giant Teacher Mill in the Sky, and how it just cranks out teachers to torment me, and how they had each devised the toughest finals known to mankind.

Right about here, the manager smiled and interrupted me, "You read scriptures every day?"

Then I told him I was a Mormon, and I told him a little bit about my daily scripture study program. He grinned even bigger and said, "Say no more. If you're a good Mormon, you're an employee I can trust. You'll be honest, you'll be punctual, and you'll help the customers find the books they want. And if you're like the last Mormon I hired, you'll even sell them some extra books that you personally recommend."

"Oh, yes sir!" I said.

"But you've got to read," he said. "Now that school's over, you can keep up with the book reviews and the bestsellers."

"Oh, easily. I mean, yes. I'll do it."

He told me when to start, and that was it! At times like these, I feel such a sense of closeness to all other members of the Church. I want to run around and thank everybody for setting a good example, and giving me a reputation that I'm proud of, a name I'm eager to live up to.

A week later, James and his family went on a vacation to Europe. His folks decided to take James and his younger sisters, since this fall James would be going on a mission and they wanted him to see Europe first. "Who knows?" said James's mother. "He could get called to serve in Oregon and then settle down and not get to see Europe for twenty years."

I know, that's who. You take a kid to Europe for those reasons, and he's sure to get a call to serve in Belgium. Mark my words, Sister

Olbern. It's exactly like washing your car and then it rains. But I said nothing.

I was sorry to see James go, though. We weren't madly in love with each other, but we had started seeing each other every week or so, and now with James gone and school over, I felt like I'd been put into cold storage for a while. I thought by working in the mall I might meet some interesting guys, but so far the only social prospects had been a ten-year-old puzzle fanatic who had a crush on me and would hang around the cash register asking me for solutions to his crossword clues, and one guy who asked me out right after he asked me where the books on guns and explosives were.

And then the stake Young Women had an activity that was their best attended ever. It was a dating panel of gorgeous guys from a different region, pulling questions out of a hat, which we girls had scribbled onto scraps of paper earlier that evening. One guy would read the question, and then they'd all respond to it. We must have looked like an audience of zombies, just staring straight at them with a level of concentration close to hypnosis. We hung on their every word as if they were the Wisdom of the Ages, laying down all the laws of dating that a girl could ever want. (In retrospect, even though it might sound corny, I've decided that's how we ought to listen to the general conference talks, not to a bunch of guys who've simply been on a dozen dates or so.)

But at the time, they had us entranced. The first guy, a definite ten in anybody's book—any country, any time—started off by talking about his "girlfriend." This left a sour expression on all of our formerly hopeful faces.

Kelly Matheson whispered, "Why does a knockout like him have to be taken?"

I sighed. "You just answered your own question," I said. Of *course* a guy that cute is going to be taken. What's amazing was that he didn't have three or four girlfriends simultaneously.

But then, as he answered a couple of the questions, I began to see him differently. When the guys were each asked to describe an ideal date, he was the only one who said that all he ever did was go to the movies. Now, movies are fun (I *love* a good movie), but if you could design a dream date, wouldn't you pick something that really helps you to get to know your date? Something that would involve more . . . I don't know . . . togetherness or something? Let's face it, as fun as movies are, each person is sort of in their own private bubble watching the movie. You could date somebody for ten years and never really get to know them if all you did was go to movies.

I'm not saying you have to contrive silly, elaborate dates. But there should be some closeness, some chance to learn about each other.

And then, when asked what subjects he most liked to talk about, this guy only shrugged and said, "I'm not much for talking." Well, I can understand a fellow being basically quiet, even shy. But this guy didn't seem very shy; he just sounded uninterested, like he didn't want much emotional contact, something that would be highly frustrating to the average female.

You know, from what I've read (thanks in part to my new job), women tend to talk more than men. In fact, they sometimes make a guy feel smothered because they want to talk so much. And some guys, very legitimately, need some silence now and then. We women would probably do well to remember that. I even read one book, written by a woman, that said it's all right to be bubbly and talkative, but that you won't be seen as very feminine if you're always yacking and telling and talking. She said silence is very alluring to a man. (Darn, I thought.)

But as I looked at this handsome panel member, I started to get the feeling that he simply didn't want to invest the effort in a normal conversation. He seemed bored. The next few questions all brought the same reaction from him: a deep sigh and a shrug, then he'd brush off the question as not really important. He didn't seem to have any energy for relationships or romance.

How interesting that by the end of the evening Kelly was whispering, "How did that guy ever get a girlfriend?" Suddenly his looks didn't matter; the shell was gorgeous but it turned out to be just that—a shell. Who knows—maybe he found that he could coast along on his looks and he never bothered to develop his personality. I guess some girls are guilty of that, too.

The other panel members were terrific. They sounded fun, bright, spiritual, and exactly like the kind of guys you never end up sitting beside at school, when the teacher makes up the seating chart. Instead, you always end up by a guy who rolls cigarettes during class, or who belches like Alvin Eisenstat, or some wolf like Charlie Pulido who wiggles his eyebrows at you all through American history (and by the time you get out of that class, you feel like you've endured him through all of history, too).

Anyway, the panel was great. One guy, Ron, was just covered with freckles, and was absolutely adorable. When he walked in, they didn't have all the chairs set up for the panel members and he obligingly sat on a radiator against one wall. Suddenly his eyes grew round and he jumped up, slapping the seat of his nearly scorched pants. We all giggled, unfortunately. It would have been better—and we probably would have sounded more datable—if we had chuckled or laughed, but no, we giggled and squealed. At least the guy was a good sport about it.

"Well, I guess my bishop was right," he said. Then he smiled. "He told me to look out, because the girls in this stake would probably put me on the hot seat."

Another fellow, Danny Martinez, drew the question, "What do you like least about dating?" and he said, "Asking a girl out who won't date me because I'm Mexican."

Suddenly, we all felt sorry for him and angry with anyone who could be so prejudiced. But then Ron put his arm around Danny and said, "Danny, you aren't really Mexican, but even if you were—so what? Nobody cares about whether someone is Mexican or not. And anyway, you just *think* you're Mexican." Then Ron looked at all of us. "See, Danny's last name is Martinez. There's just one problem. Despite doing all the genealogy they can, the Martinez family can't find a single Mexican—anywhere."

We started to laugh then, and so did Danny. "But the surname—" he insisted. "I'm sure we're Mexican."

Ron just shook his head. "Danny, Danny." We were all cracking up, now. "Danny, if a girl won't go out with you because—she has to wash her hair, let's say—" (then he winked) "maybe it's because she really does have to wash her hair."

"No," Danny said. "It's because I'm a Mexican."

Ron sighed. "What am I going to do with you, Danny?"

Danny was laughing, too, but was adamant about his excuse for getting turned down. "It's true," he said. "They don't like my culture."

Ron shook his head. "Don't be ridiculous, Danny. Anyone can see you have no culture."

Now we all howled and Danny's mouth dropped open.

"Oh, you know what I mean," Ron said, then he blushed as the other guys on the panel chuckled, enjoying Ron's embarrassment. Finally Ron cleared his throat. "No, Danny's right," he said. "I run into the same problem all the time. I'll call a girl on the phone and she'll say, 'Wait—aren't you the guy of that Icelandic/Irish extraction on one side and French/German on the other? Forget it.'"

Danny was laughing now. "Okay, so maybe it isn't because I'm Mexican. But I am Mexican."

"Okay, okay," Ron said. "We'll let you be Mexican."

"And I do get turned down for dates," Danny said.

Ron smiled. "Yeah, but it's because of that car you drive, Danny. If you can call it a car."

"Rosita?!" Danny was flabbergasted.

Ron looked at us girls. "Can you believe he named his car Rosita?" We all laughed.

Danny smiled out into the audience. "Hey. You haven't lived until you've ridden in Rosita."

"Oh, get out of here," Ron teased. "Rosita is an old Mercury Bobcat with one kind of hubcaps on the left side, and another kind on the right side."

"Hey," Danny argued, "who ever sees both sides of a car at the same time?"

By now we were howling, and when Ron said, "Who here would be willing to go out with a guy who thinks he's a Mexican and who drives a Bobcat named Rosita?" every one of us raised our hands.

Ron frowned, jealous and disgusted all at once. "Oh, boy," he said to Danny, "I can't believe how you've played upon their sympathies." Then he mimicked Danny's voice and whined, "Nobody likes me because . . . I'm European!"

Danny grinned and shrugged. "Well . . . it worked. Now, if you'll all pass your phone numbers forward . . ."

The evening went along that way, the guys a little nervous as they answered some of the tougher questions, but always with them jabbing and teasing each other. It really gave us a good chance to see what their personalities were like.

One of the questions was about morality and how they felt about a girl who was coming on pretty strong. I was so pleased to hear every one of them say that it disappointed them. Here were four guys who had their heads on straight; they had strong testimonies and they were determined to find a girl to match. You hear so much today about double standards and how so few kids maintain morals in high school these days. It was really gratifying to meet some guys who were standing strong and were proud to say so.

Mr. Looks drew the slip of paper that said, "Describe a girl who's your type." He smiled and said, "Hmm. Good looking. Tall. Slender. Blue eyes. Long legs. Tan." Then he shrugged, as if that pretty much covered it.

You should have seen us listening to him. With every adjective he ticked off, our smiles faded a notch. It was as if he were in a shooting gallery and we were little tin ducks pecking along, and he'd pop us one by one as we went by.

Then the others chimed in, wanting to add their list of favorite traits. I was glad to see the others were looking for more than physical appearance. "I like a cute laugh," one said. Sense of humor, sincerity, warmth, and common sense were also mentioned. There seemed to be an impatience with flighty, irresponsible girls and girls who put too much emphasis on clothes and make-up (for just an instant I wondered if my mom had rigged this thing).

Then they mentioned that they liked girls who had goals and dreams, who were enthusiastic about life and had given their future some thought. One guy said, "A good cook," and the others clapped. Then they all agreed that being a good friend was important, too.

Ron said, "I only date girls who are smarter than me."

"Well, sure," Danny said, "That's all there are!" We must have laughed for ten minutes as Ron squirmed, before he finally joined us in the joke.

Another question was, "What keeps you from calling a girl back, after you've had a fun date with her?"

Danny said, "If she's Mexican and she drives a Bobcat." We all laughed. Then Ron said, "If she wants to get too serious too soon." They all voiced their agreement with that. It seems that to the men, it's just a fun friendship, but to some girls it's much more and they try to pressure the guys into some kind of a commitment. Or they start hinting about marriage or children too soon.

Another reason for cooling off was sheer expense. Some of them felt that girls need to respect a guy's finances more and not always want to do the most expensive things. That's not to say that every date has to be a cheap one, but that moderation would go a long way.

The fellows also said it bugged them when their dates were always dieting. They liked a girl who could go out and order a chili dog with extra cheese, rather than half a salad every time. "It's embarrassing to sit there and eat a big meal while your date has a cup of soup," said a guy named Michael. "I like a girl who can get her hair wet, who's a good sport, who's a friend, who'll eat a big steak with me, who's loyal, and who'll back me in what I do."

"Gee, Michael," Danny said. "Sounds like you should get a German Shepherd."

After waiting for our laughter to die down, Michael turned to Danny and said, "I didn't realize this was going to be a battle of wits tonight."

Danny patted Michael on the back. "That's probably why you came unarmed." We laughed again, but Michael was a good sport.

One question was, "What do you think of meeting a girl's parents before your date?"

"Depends on the parents," Danny kidded.

"I guess I'd better like it," Ron said, "because my mom wants to meet all my dates, too."

"Oh, that sounds pretty fun," Michael said, yawning. "First you go meet her parents and talk for half an hour or so with them, then you drive over to your house and talk for a while with your parents, and then it's time for the date to end. Great evening."

With that, Brother Harris, our Designated Adult for the day, laughed and said, "Actually that's not bad preparation for what holidays will be like when you marry. You can spend your whole day paying respects to relatives and in-laws."

Ron grinned. "Well, what can I say? House rules. But after the first meeting, then we don't have to do that anymore."

Michael spoke up. "I really don't like meeting the parents. I mean, I don't mind *meeting* them, I just hate being interviewed. I wish my dates would be ready on time so I wouldn't have to be grilled for so long."

"Do they ask you if you're Mexican?" Danny said. Michael laughed and shook his head. "Actually," Danny went on, "I don't mind it when the parents ask me a lot of questions. It gives me a chance to check *them* out, too." Then Danny did a quick impersonation of a girl's father interviewing him.

"So, Mr. Marteenez, you're taking my daughter to a rock concert, eh?"

"Yes, Mr. Jones. By the way, is that a *pool* I see in your backyard?"

"Yes. Tell me, Mr. Marteenez, do you like school?"

"Why, yes, Mr. Jones. Tell me. Do you have an IRA for your daughter?"

By now we were cracking up. Danny went on and on, until finally Brother Harris had to stop him. "I think the girls who had planned to date you might have changed their minds," he said, laughing. "Mexican or not."

Then Brother Harris pulled a switch. He invited the panel to ask *us* questions, saying they could point specifically to the girls they wanted to answer them. Again, we giggled and screamed (if you don't know what to do, and you're a teenage girl, giggling and screaming seems to be the reaction of choice).

"Okay," Michael said. "What I want to know is, how come so many girls only like guys who are jerks?"

We all pretended to be baffled. Surely he didn't mean *our* well-adjusted, sensible group. And what was he talking about anyway?

He explained, "It seems like if I'm rude or late, and I don't give a girl any encouragement at all, she goes crazy for that. She'll call all the time, or she'll hang on me like I'm the greatest guy in the world. But *then,* if I really like a girl and I'm super good to her and I do everything I can for her, she dumps me." He pointed at Heather (thank goodness) to answer.

"I don't know," Heather said, thinking. "But I've seen what you're talking about. I know a lot of girls at school who have really creepy boyfriends. It doesn't make sense to me. I know that *I* really appreciate a guy who's considerate, and if someone doesn't treat me well, I usually lose interest in him."

I felt the same way. But what did explain the girls who liked bums? Brother Harris suggested that maybe these girls had poor relationships with their dads, and having a neglectful boyfriend feels secure if only because it feels familiar. It's sad, but maybe it's one explanation. Or maybe that kind of girl just likes the chase and loses interest after she's won the prize (at least, I know a lot of guys who are like this). Sometimes a girl's self-esteem will be so low that her subconscious reasoning goes kind of like that old Groucho Marx line about not wanting to belong to any club that would have him as a member. Maybe some girls feel that as soon as the guy likes her back, he must not be worth much. So on she goes to the next conquest. Or maybe those girls take nice guys for granted, mistaking their kindness for weakness. What a shame, I thought. Girls like that will probably end up in very one-sided marriages.

"Don't give in and be rude just to have those girlfriends," Brother Harris said to Michael. "Hold out and be who you really are. Be considerate and gentle and all that. Eventually you'll meet a girl who'll lap that up. You know, before I got married I saw the same thing you're describing. It used to make me mad that women were able to discard me so quickly just for being a nice guy. I almost decided to change and be a real pain. But then I thought, 'No, someday I'm going to meet the right woman who can appreciate me.' It took a while, but I did meet her, and I wouldn't have traded that for anything. I'm really glad I held out, even though I was never the Big Man on Campus."

Then he winked at the panel. "But it sounds like you have a group of girls here who already like charming men."

Of course, we clapped and hooted. Real feminine. I remember thinking, "If any one of us ever gets asked out on a date, it will be a miracle."

Then Danny raised his hand. "This isn't exactly a question," he said. "It's more like a comment. But lately I've noticed a lot of materialism in girls. It seems like they only want to date rich guys in fancy cars."

Ron groaned. "Oh, you're not blaming your *car* now, I hope! First he was a Mexican, now he's a poor Mexican. I'm telling you, some guys will do anything to get a girl to go out with them." He pointed at the audience. "Look at them, Danny. You've almost got them in tears again."

Danny laughed. "No, be serious. Don't you think girls—okay, *some* girls—judge you by how much money you have?"

Brother Harris interrupted. "Like your conversation with Mr. Jones?" he said pointedly.

"Nah, I was kidding," Danny said. "But how important is money, anyway?"

Unfortunately, he pointed at me just then. I gulped and tried to formulate an answer. "Well, uh . . . It certainly doesn't hurt to take your date out in the old Lear once in a while." Everybody laughed (thank goodness they knew I was kidding). I could feel my cheeks burning. I took a big breath. "To be honest, I can't say I wouldn't be impressed just a little bit if a guy took me on a date to, say . . . Canada." Danny laughed and watched me, waiting to hear the rest of my rambling answer. "This is really embarrassing," I whispered to Kelly, who was sitting there grinning, glad that it was me, and not her, who was on the spot.

I took a big breath. "But, on the other hand, that's just a momentary 'wow.' You have to enjoy a guy's company to go out with him again—no matter how rich he is. I mean, otherwise you're using him and that's not right. Plus, you're wasting your time on someone you know you couldn't be happy with."

Forgetting that men like women who know when to clam up, I went on, "As for dating a guy who's poor, why not? My dad always says that if you're ambitious and determined, you'll rise to the top of your field and be able to support a family no matter what your career is, so a guy who's a hard worker is more important at this age. I mean, young guys haven't had time to earn a whole lot of money, yet."

"So it's important that they have a lot of money eventually?" Danny looked right at me.

"No!" I was getting flustered. "I'm not saying that. I mean, nobody wants to struggle and be poor forever, let's face it. So, yes, he should someday have *some* money. But that doesn't mean he has to become wealthy; you just need to be comfortable. And as long as a guy knows how to manage his finances, enjoys his work, and has goals, you know that he can at least pay the bills. But for now, having a lot of money when you're young isn't something I look for. Even if a guy's family is rich, that's no guarantee he'll be hardworking. You have to evaluate each person individually, not go by how wealthy their family is. Money isn't something I think of when I decide whether to date a guy. I guess personality is more important to me."

Then Stacie Taylor raised her hand. "I like the idea of working *with* my husband to build our lifestyle together. If you marry a guy who's already made his money—unless he can somehow let you feel involved and as if you share it with him—it seems to me like walking into the middle of a movie."

"Hmm." Danny thought for a minute. "Okay, so maybe girls aren't that materialistic. Maybe it *is* that I'm Mexican." He shot a glance at Ron and we all laughed.

Then Danny looked right at me again. "Well, what about you?" he asked. "Would you go out with a guy like me?"

In one embarrassing chorus, the other girls sang, "Oooooh, Louisaaaaa!" My face must have turned every shade of purple except lavender.

Was he asking me out or just sending up a trial balloon? As I gulped and tried to find my voice, Michael said, "C'mon, Danny— there *are* no other guys like you."

Danny smiled, his eyes still fixed on mine. "True," he said without a hint of modesty. "Not every guy is a smooth, mysterious Latino."

Now Ron's palm hit the table top. "Oh, that does it!" he said, truly exasperated. "I have never seen *anybody* get so much mileage out of being Mexican in my entire life!" Now we were all laughing, more at Ron's fury than anything else. "And YOU'RE NOT EVEN MEXICAN!" He looked half ready to strangle Danny, when Michael stood up behind him and patted his shoulders. "C'mon, Ron, relax," he said. "You know cheaters never prosper."

Now Ron whirled around at Michael and cast him a look that promptly sent Michael back to his chair without further "comforting" clichés.

Danny was eating it up. And . . . still waiting for my answer. "Sure," I said. (Two minutes to think, and that's the best I could mumble.)

"Well, how about this Friday night?"

I felt dizzy and more embarrassed now than ever. "I . . . I can't Friday night," I said.

OKAY, SHOOT ME. I LIED. I WAS NO MORE BUSY FRIDAY NIGHT THAN THE STUFFED ARMADILLO AT THE MUSEUM OF SCIENCE AND INDUSTRY WAS. But there was no way I was going to admit in front of all these people that I was *that* available. Accuse me of playing games and I can only plead guilty.

"The next Friday night?" Danny asked.

"Okay," I said. Everyone around me seemed to be nudging me and yelping and making remarks, and at this point, I would have agreed to a beheading. I just wanted the focus of attention to go somewhere else.

Thank goodness Brother Harris intervened at that moment. "Danny, how about you arrange that later? We need to move along. Who else would like to ask a question of the ladies?"

Ron had calmed down, now, and just shook his head at Danny one last time. "Okay," he said, "I've got a question. What is it women want?"

The room erupted into chatter and Brother Harris had to silence all the girls who were shouting, "You'll do fine!" and the like. (Were we raised in *barns* or what?)

Then Ron continued, "Seriously. How do you make a woman happy?"

Well, he knocked my socks off with that question. Just the fact that he asked it, just seeing that he really wanted to know how to make someone else happy, impressed me to pieces. Even Brother Harris said, "Ron, something tells me you'll have no problem making a woman very happy. *Wanting* to is probably the key to it."

I almost blurted out, "You said it!" But common sense told me to be quiet; I'd already blabbered enough.

"Let's toss this one out to the whole group," Brother Harris said. "Girls?"

Then we all started thinking aloud and shouting suggestions as Brother Harris wrote them on the board. Finally we consolidated them into four simple techniques that we "women" agreed upon and that I thought sounded incredibly easy.

If guys would only realize how simple it is, they'd have women wrapped around their fingers all the time. The trouble is that the formula goes against the basic nature of some guys. Here are the four components: Talk to her, listen to her, make her laugh, and touch her a lot.

So many guys have a hard time opening up and sharing themselves in a conversation. Yet women eat this up! When you say to a guy, "Let's talk," and you mean, let's just share and visit together, his first thought is, "What do you want to talk about?" He's thinking like the Chairman of the Board and expects you to announce a specific topic.

But you, being a woman, say "Oh, nothing in particular." So then he, thoroughly baffled by this, just shakes his head and mutters, "Women!"

On the subject of listening, what a woman really wants is for her man to look back at her and respond. In actual words, not occasional grunts. She wants some verbal feedback, some eye contact, and will be thrilled beyond description if the guy goes so far as to ask her questions and truly, actively listen. But a lot of guys figure that an occasional "hmph" will keep the conversation going (and lots of women will talk indefinitely anyway), so that's all they offer. They think they are satisfying the woman because she keeps on talking. But then she keeps on talking because she's hoping she'll someday utter the sentence that gets a response out of him. (They're both wrong.)

On making her laugh, I can think of almost nothing as intoxicating as sharing laughter and fun with someone you love. This doesn't mean your boyfriend has to be a standup comic; only that he should be able to look at the light side of things and be able to laugh at himself.

Touching is important, too. The kind I'm talking about is squeezing a girl's hand, or caressing her neck, maybe just stroking her back, or running his hands through your hair. Am I right? You'd give anything if every guy in the world could learn those four tricks, right?

To us it seems so easy because that's how women are. Who knows? Not being a man, I don't know what kind of a list they might have like that. Probably something like, "Don't make me talk so much, don't you talk so much, don't put so much importance on laughing, and don't ask me to get physical and then get mad when I try to take it farther than you want to."

I guess that's just the way the world is. (Although my mom and dad seem to have a really good friendship, and I see both of them trying to please the other in the ways I just mentioned. Sometimes I know my mom is dying to talk to my dad, but she lets him unwind and have some space first, and sometimes I know my dad is really too tired to talk, but he goes to my mom and asks questions and holds her and even gets her laughing.) So it *is* possible to get together on this thing.

Soon the time was up and the panel had to leave for parts unknown, geographic regions that we figured were too remote for any of them to consider us as other than G. U. (Geographically Unsuitable). Except for Danny's bold invitation to me, we figured that was the last we'd see of the Panel Men. But the experience helped us understand dating from a male perspective, and most of us learned a great deal.

Naturally I took a jeep-load of ribbing from the incident, and one girl (gee, why is there always one?) even hinted that Danny was probably just showing off in front of Ron, with whom he seemed to have a running competition.

"Yeah, that's probably all it was," I said. "After all, why on earth would anyone be *serious* about dating Louisa Barker?"

Then she quickly said, "Oh, I didn't mean it that way." But I just smiled. We both knew she did, only this time I had the sense to say something, instead of slithering home to lick my wounds the way I usually do when my overly sensitive feelings get bruised like that. (I'm usually so surprised and caught off guard, that I can't even think of what to say for a day or two.)

Still, it planted seeds of doubt and I began to wonder if Danny would be calling to back out. I replayed the conversation in my mind to see if maybe he was just being a little cocky, a little strident, and before he knew it, got cornered into asking me out when he really didn't want to.

Finally a little voice inside me said, "Knock it off! You're acting insecure and even a little bit stupid. He asked you out because he wants to take you out. Now stop worrying."

So I did.

CHAPTER THREE
Louisa's Nose Grows

The next few days were so busy at the bookstore, I hardly had time to think about Danny and our upcoming date. Okay, that's not entirely the truth.

Let me try this again. Despite being busy on my new job, I thought about my upcoming date with Danny almost constantly. Yes. Much better and much more honest.

It wasn't that I was infatuated with him; it was that I was nervous. The only guys I had ever dated were fellows I already knew pretty well from school, church, or whatever. But Danny and I had never even had one private conversation. What if we got out on our date and had nothing in common and nothing to say to each other? I didn't know the first thing about him or his family or any of his feelings. On the other hand, I figured this complete lack of information might give us plenty to talk about.

"Louisa." A strong male voice penetrated my daydream like the thud of a box of books right in front of me. In fact, it *was* the thud of a box of books in front of me. My boss, Mr. Cooper, had asked me to shelve some new arrivals, and now he had caught me daydreaming.

"Oh—I'm so sorry," I said. And then I thought, wait a minute. This isn't like me to space out like that. I am not a flaky kid. So I decided to tell him what I'd been thinking about.

"I'm usually not like that," I said. "It's just that—" I took a big breath. "At church a few days ago, we had this dating panel."

Mr. Cooper—who was chewing on the end of a pipe which he never lit and which I suspect he just carried around as a prop, to look bookish or something—just kept chewing and raised one eyebrow. "A what?"

I grinned and lowered my voice. "A dating panel—you know, a bunch of guys sit at this panel and answer girls' questions about dating."

Mr. Cooper was now trying to stifle a smile and be businesslike, but I could just tell he wanted me to go on. At least I think that's what he was thinking.

"So one of the guys asked me out—right in the middle of the discussion—in front of everybody!"

Now Mr. Cooper was frowning that fatherly frown we've all seen, and said, "Well! I certainly hope you said no. You don't want to look desperate in front of everyone."

Horrors! I had looked desperate in front of everyone! Or was he kidding? I just hate it when I can't tell if a grown-up is using some kind of subtle sarcasm or if they're truly shocked by what you're saying. Was I worrying unnecessarily—is that what he was trying to tell me? Or had I really made a fool of myself, looking like an easy mark in front of the entire Young Women's organization?

"Ha—desperate? Me?" I rolled my eyes as if the very idea were the height of ridiculousness. "Of course I turned him down. I mean, the guy wasn't even attractive. What kind of a guy asks you out like that, anyway?"

I turned to get back to work and nearly bumped smack into Danny Martinez. To say that I gasped is to say that Monstro the Whale gave a little sneeze in Pinocchio. And speaking of that lying little puppet, I felt my nose should be at least as long as his by now.

"Danny! Oh—uh—" I wanted to die.

Danny, of course, had walked up behind me and had heard the entire conversation. I don't know who was blushing more, him or me. He didn't say anything; he just looked at me like a wounded puppy.

"Oh, Danny! Uh, this is my boss, Mr. Cooper."

Mr. Cooper nodded. "You a friend of Louisa's?"

Danny gave me a cold glance. "Well, I thought I was." Then he walked out of the bookstore.

My knees were trembling and I turned back to Mr. Cooper, who now realized that his "good Mormon" employee had just lied to him, right through her teeth.

"Mr. Cooper, could I please have just fifteen minutes to try to explain things?"

"With him or with me?"

Yikes! Another decision! No doubt I would flub this one, too. "Danny?" I guessed.

Mr. Cooper shook his head. "That was the boy on the panel?"

"Yes—oh, I am so embarrassed and so sorry. I really feel so stupid. I . . . I was ashamed to tell you that I had made a date with him after all. I mean, you seemed so sure that a girl who did that was desperate, and I didn't want you to think that I did a dumb thing—"

"Unlike this moment, for example?"

"Yes—I wasn't honest and I feel terrible about that. Honest." Oh, why does my brain fail me when I need it most?

Mr. Cooper smiled, then sighed. "Go on. Fifteen minutes."

"Oh, thank you," I shouted as I bolted out of the store.

I looked frantically for Danny, who had evidently vanished into thin air. Maybe he had been translated, as a reward for having just been mercilessly humiliated by a girl whose ability to make a guy feel like a million bucks is surpassed only by her missionary skills in impressing her nonmember boss.

Everyone in malldom seemed to be walking as slowly as they possibly could, and all of them were maneuvering their wide bottoms and strollers right into my path.

Oh, this is just great, I thought. I can see the headlines in tomorrow's paper. WHITNEY HIGH GRADUATE ARRESTED— Honors Student Goes Berserk in Mall, Tramples Family of Five.

Film crews would cluster around me as they led me away, handcuffed and head bowed. Two or three reporters would shove microphones into my face. "Louisa, why did you do it? Was it really to cover up a double lie?"

Tears streaming down my face, and hair caught in my mouth (with handcuffs on, how could I pull it out?), I would look up and say, "No—I was trying to tell the truth!"

The reporters would all shake their heads. "Yeah, yeah. You and Charles Manson."

Then they'd cut to a film clip of Mr. Cooper. "I guess you never can tell about people," he'd say, chewing on his pipe. "She seemed like such a nice girl, too. A Mormon, in fact."

Zing—there I'd be—a Mormon criminal! Just like all those other spies and hijackers who would fade into oblivion except that (drum roll, here) they happen to be Mormons, a juicy piece of information the media seizes upon and worms into every headline they can.

Next they'd show Danny, leaning against the front door of the Foreign Legion. His eyes would hold the hurt of a whole nation, and he'd say, "You know, I thought I could trust Louisa. I've never had anyone be so cruel and humiliate me so completely. I'll never be the same."

Next, a shot of my parents, wearing black. My mother would be bent over, sobbing, while my dad was trying to hold her up and walk her along. Through her hysteria, Mom would be mumbling, "Where did we go wrong, Gordon?" and Dad would be waving the film crews away, saying, "Not now, not now" to them.

My heart was pounding as I ran through the mall. Where did all these crowds come from? This was worse than the Christmas Crunch. Finally I darted down a side wing and saw Danny just pushing on the exit door.

"Danny—wait!" I screamed.

Some junior high guys, trying to impress each other, were sitting at an Orange Julius bar, and mimicked me. "Danny, wait!" one of them said, in a tinny little voice.

I spun around. "Hey. You got a problem with that, Jack?" I yelled. Suddenly I gulped. What was I doing? This was mild-mannered, okay— medium-mannered Louisa Barker? Had I completely lost my mind?

Danny walked up beside me. "Are you one of those fighting chicks?" he asked. He sounded serious, like a customer in a tropical fish store asking if those are the fighting fish.

"No!" I was panting, half-exhausted from running all over the mall and half-exhausted from the adrenaline of my arrest fantasy.

"Well, what are you trying to do—pick a fight with those guys?" Danny gestured toward the Orange Julius stand, where—thank goodness—the guys were leaving.

"Danny, I know what you're thinking. You're thinking I'm some loud-mouthed, stupid girl and you're glad you found this out because no way do you want to go out with some girl who's going to yell stupid things at people and who's going to get you into fights and stuff and that's not how I am, really. I'm just so upset and so sorry and embarrassed and I—please forgive me, Danny, because what I said back there—"

Danny was making the time-out sign with his hands now and led me over to the Orange Julius stand to sit down.

"Here. I'll buy. You need to calm down."

"No, I'm okay. Those drinks are half air, anyway—the top half, you know?"

Danny just stared at me. "What are you talking about?"

"You know, how they whip up all that foam on the tops of the drinks." I said breathlessly, still in a panic.

Danny got me some ice water and felt my forehead.

"I am so sorry, Danny—that was all a big lie—" I started again. "I do think you're cute or I wouldn't have said yes—"

"Louisa?"

"Yes?"

"Just drink the water."

So we sat there quietly for a couple of minutes. Finally I explained it all to Danny. I told him that my original intention was just to let my boss know why I was daydreaming, but that after discovering my boss's views, I wanted him to think I felt the same way.

"But why do you care what your boss thinks?" Danny asked.

"Are you kidding? I care what everybody thinks," I said. "I'm embarrassed almost eighty percent of the time."

Danny laughed. "You've got to be your own person, Louisa. Stand up for yourself. There was nothing wrong with accepting a date during that panel."

"Yeah, I guess you're right. Boy, that was so cheap and little of me. I really apologize."

Danny smiled. "Well, I'm glad you caught up with me. I was drawing some pretty unfair conclusions."

"Like what?"

"See? There you go again. It's all straightened out now, Louisa. You can stop worrying about what I think, what you think, what your boss thinks—"

"Oh, my gosh—Mr. Cooper!" I checked my watch. "I was supposed to be back there five minutes ago. He'll fire me! Plus I've still got to explain all this to him, too."

Danny smiled and walked back with me. "You'll do fine."

"So—are we—do you still—"

Danny laughed. "Sure—that's why I came into your store, y'know. I called your house and your mom said you were working. Is six-thirty okay? I have a surprise planned. Do you have a formal dress you can wear?"

"Sure," I said, just relieved to be forgiven.

By now we were back at the bookstore, and I dashed in to catch Mr. Cooper. He had finished unpacking the books and before I could even say anything, he pointed to some customers for me to help. It was about an hour before I had a minute to talk to him.

After I explained it all, and admitted worrying about what he would think of me, he chuckled. "You got yourself into a good one, Louisa," he said.

"I hope you don't think I take honesty lightly," I said. "You'd never have to worry about me stealing from the register or anything—"

"I know," he said. "And Louisa, I was only kidding about looking desperate. I was just making a joke."

"Oh." I tried to force a smile, but I'm sure it looked as weak as I felt by now. "Heh. That was a good one, Mr. Cooper."

I took a big breath and Mr. Cooper patted me on the back. "Relax, Louisa. Things can only get better now."

"Yeah," I said. "I'm glad that episode is over with."

"By the way," Mr. Cooper said, "speaking of dating, I know a young Mormon fellow I want to introduce you to. I think the two of you would be perfectly suited to each other. You're both avid readers, good students, the same religion—you interested?"

I brightened, always open to new ideas. "Sure!" 1 said. "Who is it—the employee you said used to work here?"

Mr. Cooper smiled. "Yes—that's the one. His name is Mark Davis. Ever heard of him?"

CHAPTER FOUR

Dating: Whose Idea Was This, Anyway?

You know, sometimes I wonder if maybe a sense of humor is, like, essential for salvation or something. I mean, obviously God knows what's going on here: He knows Mark Davis is the rock in my gym shoe of life. And he knows I got myself into a knee-deep mess with that dumb lie about Danny Martinez. And I figure He is either looking down on this pathetic little scene absolutely cracking up in gales of laughter (calling various pals over to watch me squirm), or He's holding a clipboard and marking off how well I am able to roll with unbelievable punches.

I don't mean any of that to sound sacrilegious. I know my Heavenly Father loves me to pieces, more than I can comprehend. But that's the whole point, you know? It's like—I know my dad loves me and when he ribs me or teases me, it's because he knows me sometimes better than I know myself. Don't you ever feel like sometimes God nudges you a little bit and grins? It seems like He sometimes gives us little "gotchas" to keep us humble.

This was one of those times, when I wanted to look up into the heavens and say, "Thou thinkest this is funny, doesn't thou?" I mean, here was Mr. Cooper (who had been joking, of all things, about that dating panel, only I didn't know that), now standing quite seriously in front of me, telling me that the perfect guy for me is Marky Davis, Brat Emeritus.

I could feel myself slipping over the edge into uncontrolled hysteria. Should I strangle Mr. Cooper? Should I lie again and say, "Oh, yes—I know who Mark is. Seems like a great guy." Or should I fall to the floor, pound the ground, and plead for mercy?

I started laughing. The whole irony of it all, the ridiculous timing of Danny hearing me put him down, the insane predicament of lying to my new boss, the crazy odds of the former employee being Mark Davis—the whole wild, exhausting, impossible day this had been, was just too much for my wee little body to hold, and the excess simply spilled out in roaring laughter.

"I take it you already know Mark?"

I wiped my damp eyes. "Well," I said, trying to catch my breath, "I know who he is. I rode in a teacup with him once."

Now Mr. Cooper was looking at me with serious doubt in his eyes, as to my mental state. "I thought Mormons didn't drink tea," he finally said.

"It was at Disneyland."

"Oh. You can drink tea at Disneyland?"

I sighed. I was so tired of miscommunicating. I looked at Mr. Cooper, his tan cardigan, his sensible shoes. I could tell he didn't know the first thing about the Magic Kingdom.

"Mr. Cooper," I said, as patiently as I could. "The teacups are a ride at Disneyland."

"Oh—then you've already dated Mark?"

"No! I was out with someone else at the time."

Mr. Cooper frowned. "Then why were you riding the teacups with Mark Davis?"

Because the universe is full of cruel jokes, I thought to myself. Because I have nothing better to do than spend Grad Night assuring James Olbern that I don't have a crush on Mark Davis. Because I'm in a bad biorhythm and my luck at present includes getting stuffed into a blender with a guy who wears popcorn-box hats when he goes to the movies.

"Things just happen," I said. "Don't ask me why."

Mr. Cooper smiled. "Well, if you already know him, there's no sense in my trying to arrange a date for you."

I sighed. "Thanks anyway."

Mr. Cooper smiled, a cute Grandpa sort of smile, and went back to work. I took a big breath, closed my eyes, and said a quick prayer. I apologized for lying, I thanked God for helping the whole thing to finally smooth over, and then I asked Him to please give me a break and let the rest of the day go uneventfully.

When I opened my eyes, there stood Ron, another guy from the panel. I blinked. Was I seeing things?

"Hi," Ron said.

Ho boy. Okay, so not all our prayers are answered as we would want. When I asked for the rest of the day to be easy, the answer was no. Or maybe God just snickered a bit.

"Ron! What are you doing here?" I asked.

"Well, I called your house and your mom said you were working."

Oh, I can't wait to hear my folks tonight. "What did you *do* at that dating panel, Louisa? Claim to be an heiress? Ha-ha-ha." No doubt Mom had already called Bill, Darin, and Barbara, my older siblings who think my dating is "just so cute," and they're all giggling over the idea of two or three guys walking into the bookstore all at once, and me being embarrassed to the hilt. Now all I needed was for James Olbern to come back from Europe, and decide that this very minute is the time for him to buy a couple of new paperbacks.

As a matter of fact, I'm surprised Ron wasn't just an hour or two earlier. He could have bumped into Danny and then *both* of them could have heard my cowardly lie about the panel.

"Well—it's good to see you again," I said. "Danny was in earlier." This time I was leaving no room for deception or misunderstanding.

"I know. Your mom thought I was him calling back again." Why can't moms be cool? Why can't they tell one guy's voice from another's? Why, when a guy calls, can't they just *ask* who it is instead of guessing a bunch of wrong names and humiliating you to death? Am I going to do this to my daughter someday—is it an unavoidable law of motherhood or something?

"Well, you know moms." I shrugged.

"Yep. Mine is the same way. So this is where you work." I smiled, thinking about all the fast comebacks a person could rattle off (No, I just love the nametags at this store). But poor Ron seemed so nervous, and being no stranger to sweaty palms, I just smiled. "Mmm-hmm. I like books, so I figured maybe a bookstore would be a fun summer job before I go off to BYU."

Ron looked around, shoving his hands into his pockets. "Oh, you're going to BYU?" He seemed aware that he was asking obvious questions, and I wanted so much to tell him to just relax. He had seemed so confident during the panel; why was he so nervous now?

"Yes," I said. "How about you?"

"I'm waiting for my mission papers. After that, I'm thinking about a school back East. I want to study law, I think."

"BYU has a good law school."

"Well, I've got this . . . scholarship."

"That's great! And you can use it after your mission?"

"I'm checking on that now. Listen, I know you're busy working . . ."

I glanced around for Mr. Cooper. He was with a customer. Ron took a deep breath. "Listen, would you like to go out Friday night?"

"You mean Friday night next week? Because that's when I have that date with Danny—"

"No. I mean in two days."

I blinked. "Two days? But . . . remember Danny asked me that night and I said I was busy."

"Yeah, but your mom told me you don't have anything planned," Ron grinned. "I didn't ask her; she volunteered it."

I could feel my face burning with embarrassment again, and no way was I going to cover up one lie with yet another. I sighed. "Okay, it's true. I wasn't busy."

Now Ron was confident again. "Hey, I don't blame you for saying you were busy. I know how girls are."

"Oh, you do?"

"Sure. After that panel, I'm an expert on girls."

"Really? Do you have any idea how embarrassed a girl is when her mother volunteers private information? Did she happen to tell you that I forgot to make my bed this morning, too? Any baby stories about me that I might have miss—"

Ron laughed. "Relax." Me relax? I thought *he* was supposed to be the nervous one. "Moms just talk."

No kidding.

"So will you go out with me?"

Mr. Cooper was heading my way now and overheard Ron's question. "Let me guess," he said, intruding all over the place and really embarrassing me. "Another panel member?"

"Hey, how does he know about the panel?" Ron asked.

"That must have been quite an evening," Mr. Cooper said. He had this smug little smile on his face, like a rascal uncle whose sole joy in life comes from picking on nieces and nephews.

"Mr. Cooper," I whined. "I promise I didn't plan any of this. I'm trying to work hard, honest I am—"

But that didn't seem to be Mr. Cooper's worry. He almost seemed to enjoy my agony. "Oh, don't apologize, Louisa. I had no idea that in hiring you I'd be bringing in so many new customers." Oh, terrific—make it sound like guys just swarm in here by the dozens.

Now Ron could sense that I was beginning to associate pain and humiliation with the dating panel, so he made a hasty exit, promising to call me later. Mr. Cooper spent the remainder of the afternoon glancing over at me and chuckling to himself.

That night, true to form, my siblings called to tease me and ask about "the new guys."

"What about James?" Bill asked. "What if he finds out?"

"What do you mean 'finds out'?" I said. "This isn't something sneaky, Bill. James and I aren't engaged, you know. He's just a friend. I'm not trying to hide this."

"Don't you care about hurting other people's feelings?"

I sighed. "No. It runs in the family!"

"Whoa, are you touchy!" Bill said. "These guys must be pretty special."

Then Barbara called. "So did they walk in at the same time?" She sounded almost hopeful.

"No," I said.

Her voice sank. "Oh."

Then Darin called. "How did you finagle this one, sis? Two in the bookstore at one time, both asking you out? How'd you do it?"

"Hey, Darin," I said. "Stuff it."

"Louisa!" Mom called from the kitchen. "What on earth is the matter with you?"

I covered the receiver. "C'mon, Mom—everyone's giving me a hard time."

Now Dad, one finger marking his page in a news magazine, came strolling in. "Oh, Louisa, take a joke. You've always been such a good sport."

I spoke into the receiver again. "Darin," I said, "I think I'll wash my hair now."

Darin was snickering on the other end. "Gotta get ready for all those dates, eh?"

"Right." I hung up. Mom and Dad were both standing there, staring at me. "You sure you know what you're doing?" Dad asked.

"Oh, please," I said, "if I knew what I was doing, I wouldn't be doing any of this."

"What does that mean?" Mom asked.

"I have no idea," I said as I walked out of the kitchen, exhausted from the day's events. Everything and everyone seemed to be descending on me, and all I wanted was just to work at a summer job and earn a few bucks so I could buy some clothes at BYU. Was that asking so much?

I slumped down onto the sofa and tried to remember the days when I felt so sorry for myself because I didn't have a date. A few minutes later the phone rang. "Not interested," I shouted toward the kitchen, sure that it was Darin again with some inane comment.

"It's Kelly," Mom called.

I couldn't decide whether I had the energy to relate the day's disasters to Kelly, but it turned out she'd already heard about most of them through Brother Harris, with whom *both* Danny and Ron had talked today. He also home teaches Kelly's family (and what an inspiring visit that must have been).

"So who do you like best?" she asked.

I sighed. "Mr. Cooper," I said. We both laughed. "I don't know. Do I have to decide right now?" I was beginning to wish I had never even attended panel night.

"No. But you *have* to let me know how the dates go."

I promised. After all, what are best friends for?

I decided I'd better start thinking about my date with Ron since it was coming up in just two days. That didn't leave much time for brooding over the inevitable grilling my dad would put him through when he came to pick me up. Knowing Darin, he'd be on hand too, under the guise of just dropping in—only he and I would know it was to check out my date. He'd be unable to resist dragging ancient history out into the living room and relating some story about how I wet my pants the first time I went trick-or-treating (age three), and how it made all the colors in my clown suit run together. Of course he would leave out the small detail that it was himself in a vampire costume with fake blood dripping from his chin, who leaped out from behind a bush and scared me out of my wits that evening.

After Ron had been thus entertained and enlightened, we'd have to head over to his house to meet the Farnsworth family. And wasn't Ron the panel member who'd said his mom had to meet all of his dates? I could hardly wait for *that* inspection.

It makes you wonder about the whole concept of dating.

Whose idea was this, anyway? Where did the notion come from—medieval days when the torture chambers were full? I can see a round-bellied king pounding his staff on the castle floor to sentence some poor booby to the dungeon—but suddenly a court aide, wearing puffy sleeves and leotards, whispers in the king's ear, "Dungeons are all full, Sire."

The king would huff and bluster for a few seconds and then he'd stop—a light bulb going off in his mind. Okay—a candle in those days. But an idea, nonetheless. He'd whisper back to the aide, then gather his advisors together and they'd all giggle at the deliciously evil scheme the king had just hatched.

The king would wave away his yes-men, who would scurry to their places along the red carpet. Then the king would clear his throat. "I sentence you . . . ," he would boom slowly, "to spend five years . . . DATING."

All the aides, who now understood the concept, would groan sympathetically with the accused loyal subject, and the subject would say, "Pardon me, Your Highness."

The king would then assign some lackey to explain it to the guy, and the poor peasant would traipse sadly out the door, wishing there had been just one more vacancy in the dungeons.

From that day forward, dating was something inflicted primarily upon unruly teenagers who typically sneered at the royals. In time, *all* teenagers fell victim to the practice, and within two or three centuries, society had convinced itself that dating was in fact necessary, an essential step to marriage.

Parents in stone cottages would advise their youngsters about the practice, and girls, most especially, would record breathless entries into their Olde English diaries, actually expressing eager anticipation of the ordeal.

History would see thousands of young people courting, riding in horse-drawn carriages, and sticking themselves with the pins of countless corsages and boutonnieres. Carrier pigeons would transport love notes. Women would begin waving white hankies as they bid their beaus good-bye at train stations and shipyards. The telephone would be invented and boys would begin calling girls to invite them on dates. Girls would sit beside said telephones and actually wait for such calls. Some girls would even begin to call some boys.

And before you know it, there would be a dating panel in some ward building in the United States, where squealing teenage girls would ask complete strangers how to date. Two of those strangers would select one girl to zero in on, and she would become the helpless quarry in their hunt for a maiden who can drink an entire 7-Up without belching. Would she pass the test? Or would she simply pass out?

I'm not saying I've never had a fun date. I have. After I got used to it and the nervousness subsided, I've honestly enjoyed most of the dates I've been on. But the concept is still bizarre. You arrange to spend time with someone under the pretense that you are getting to know them. Unfortunately, the stuff dates are made of (contrived evenings unlike anything you'd do at home, for example) tell you almost nothing about the other person. You both try to make a good impression and the best you can offer when you're young and inexperienced is an attempt to be your best self—whatever that is—and of course you conceal your flaws, if you can. This way, both people think they are getting to know a real person, when in fact they are only becoming familiar with the image the other person decides to present at the moment. Some people even think they are falling in love with this image.

What happens to people who get married and then find out they married a completely different person than the one who was always ready at seven o'clock on Friday nights? Who is this woman in curlers and this man in a bathrobe?

I don't know. It seems there must be a better way. (It isn't living together. Not only does that break a number of commandments, but people who do that have the same divorce rate as everybody else.)

I like to do fun things as a group in order to get to know guys—say, everybody goes hiking or acts in a school musical, pitches in on some service project, or plays certain sports or games together. That way, you start out with the advantage of being in a real situation, a natural gathering of people with some reason to be together. The opportunity to be false seems diminished, expectations and pressures seem relaxed, and it even seems more fun.

Not that I don't love a dressy, romantic evening. But those seem more appealing after you already know each other well. I want to date my future husband regularly and keep our romance strong after we're married. I know it can be done, if you both agree to make it a priority. My folks do this. Every week they have a date night. Sometimes they go to the temple, sometimes they take in a movie. And frequently one of them will plan a surprise for the other. Mom likes concerts and Dad likes to attend ball games. So they each compromise and try to please the other.

They both like to eat out, so they've formed a club of sorts—more like a group of people who are all basically "foodies"—and they call it CROAK. It stands for Cheap Restaurants Of All Kinds. Once a month, Mom and Dad go out with a bunch of friends to a new restaurant. It has to be inexpensive so that everyone can afford to go and so that they can continue to pursue this Cheap Food Dream twelve times a year. And they have a blast, just trying out places where they've never been and visiting with each other.

I'm not anxious to get married, but I do look forward to the time when I can date a husband I am deeply in love with, someone with whom I have a shared history and lots of warm memories, someone I've been married to and have raised children with, someone who dates me because he genuinely enjoys my company, and someone with whom I can absolutely be myself without worrying about getting acquainted. Married life sounds so terrific; I guess that's why most of us endure the dating life. There just doesn't seem to be another way to get to know potential mates. It really comes down to No Guts, No Glory. If you don't have the guts to date—even if some dates are miserable—then you'll never taste the glory of finding your celestial partner.

Wouldn't it be great if you didn't have to date and you could just get married—and *then* date your husband? The trick is knowing which person to marry.

Other cultures seem to handle it pretty well. In those countries where they arrange marriages, you see far fewer divorces than you do in the U.S. In some faraway lands they make you have chaperones until you're married. This doesn't seem like such a bad idea (as long as my brother Darin wouldn't be the chaperone). If the date started to get dull, you could always strike up a conversation with the chaperone.

Some tribes have a custom I like: the guy who likes you comes over, but he has to be accompanied by a cluster of his buddies, who then proceed to rib and tease the daylights out of him. This way the prospective bride gets to see a very important trait: can this fellow laugh at himself and be easygoing, or is he a hothead and a crybaby? Well, that's not exactly how it was worded in the book I read for a social studies class, but you get the idea.

Sometimes we hear of cultures where the mate selection process is very different, and simply because it is different, we wrinkle our noses and declare that we could never survive in such a primitive place.

But I wonder what some of these people would think of our methods. They'd probably laugh until their sides hurt. Look at our divorce rates. Look at how complicated we've made the male/female relationship. They would undoubtedly blame our wacky dating system for at least part of that. (You know, in some cultures they never go through teenage traumas or adolescent rebellions because they have a specific day when your childhood ends and bingo! you're an instant adult. Don't tell me they aren't onto something.)

I can see a present-day Margaret Mead visiting our culture and writing a book called *Coming of Age in a Shakey's Pizza Parlor.* What would she have to say about the strange female custom of going to the bathroom en masse? What about the awkward ritual of the goodnight kiss, or the gamey way I told Danny I was busy on that first Friday night?

How about the way we dodge each other in school hallways, if we don't want to start rumors about being a "couple"? Or the way we send messages through our girlfriends to see if someone likes us? And imagine what an anthropologist would say about girls who try on five different outfits before settling on the one they're going to wear to a car-washing fund-raiser.

Picture a sociologist trying to explain why a carload of girls drives by some guy's house in order to see him, and then when they do in fact see him, they all scream, then screech out of there as if seeing him was the last thing they wanted.

You talk about strange customs—how about couples who pretend to be parking to look at the city lights, but who soon steam up their windows in other pursuits? And the common practice of partying with drugs and alcohol (hopefully not among LDS kids) would probably rank right up there with the custom some tribes have of blowing herbs up one another's noses through a length of bamboo.

No, dating is not something that comes naturally. At least, not the way it's usually done. I hope someday I have the chance to really get to know a guy—not just by going dancing or whatever, but by working alongside him or being his friend first. It's the only way I can think to determine who he really is. And who I am, too. After all, one reason to date is to learn about yourself, not just to learn about the other person.

I thought about my upcoming dates with Ron and Danny. After a day like today, I figured that both they and I had already learned enough about Louisa (and that lying doesn't pay).

Now, with any luck, the focus could shift to them, and I'd have a chance to see what they were like. I smiled to myself; maybe we'd actually have some fun.

CHAPTER FIVE
Friday Night Follies

Well, yes and no. (Kind of like the answers to certain prayers.) I had fun with Ron—at least I thought I did—until I went on the same exact date with Danny. And this was no mere coincidence, such as going to the same movie twice. Both of these guys called and told me to dress formally, then they took me bowling.

Let me explain. In Ron and Danny's ward, they had just had a seminar on innovative dating. Some clown—pardon me, some "older and wiser" guy—sat all the young men down afterwards (not at church, but in his own home and definitely not with church approval) and gave them a list of dates that had to spring from the mind of a caged toucan.

He even suggested a series of dates to go on, in order to "test" girls for important qualities (insanity would have been helpful, for example). First, he said, you tell the girl to get all dressed up, then you take her bowling or to a rodeo. This is to test her sense of humor and to see whether she's a good sport. (Don't throw up yet; it gets worse.)

For the second date, you're to tell her to wear grubbies. Now you can see if she is trusting or suspicious. Will she do as instructed and dress casually? Or will she recall your last shenanigans and do the opposite? (How these guys expect to *get* a second date escapes me.) If she trusts you and wears grubbies, she passes the test. (She also qualifies to compete in an I.Q. test with a chicken.) Take her out for a taco.

On the third date, you ask her to cook for you. This is to test her homemaking skills and also to see what kind of family she comes from. Peek into her bedroom, this guy said, to see if she'll be a neat housekeeper.

On the fourth date, you let her watch you do something, say, play in a ballgame. This is to see if she's supportive and willing to cheer you on.

The list went no further, and it didn't need to. Whatever you do for subsequent dates with such a doormat wouldn't really matter, because you are, after all, dating a turnip.

When I went on the date with Ron I figured he was just trying to be funny and do something novel. I went along with it. And anyway, my long dress was actually a tad short and bowling shoes instead of heels turned out to be the perfect height.

I still think Ron is a basically nice guy who is too nervous and self-conscious to simply date and be himself. I guess he felt comfortable with a structured plan, especially coming from an older guy he admired (and who has since been sternly reprimanded for encouraging guys to behave so foolishly).

It didn't dawn on me that I was being graded in some kind of elaborate examination until my date with Danny was exactly the same. As soon as we pulled up to the bowling alley, I turned to him and said, "Danny, what's going on here?"

When I told him about Ron, Danny leveled with me and spilled the whole plan.

"Did it ever occur to you that this older man might just be toying with you guys? Just to see if you'd do it?" I asked.

Danny was embarrassed. He hadn't thought of that. He said that the whole thing had just seemed like harmless fun.

"Yes, but now I feel used," I said. "It was . . . deceptive." Plus it implies that girls are desperately seeking the approval of every guy in town and that they have to go through all kinds of gymnastics to audition for the role of wife. Even more, the plan assumes that the girl alone must "prove" herself, while the guy simply sits back like a judge at the Olympics and scores her performance.

Danny seemed really ashamed. But he also pointed out that now we were even, and I agreed that—considering my bookstore blunder—we'd each been less than honest. "Can we start over?" he asked. "I really do like you."

I agreed.

Danny looked chagrined. "Well, with you all dressed up I guess I can't exactly take you out for a hamburger."

I grinned. "No, I guess not."

"Serves me right," he sighed and started Rosita up again. Then he took me to one of the more elegant restaurants in town.

Over the summer Danny and I have gone out a few more times, and we've always had a good time. It's kind of like we know we're keeping each other honest and game-free. It feels great to see him and know that whatever we're saying or doing is how we really feel.

Once he came to get me for a church barbecue party, and I wasn't quite ready when I opened the door. I could hear Rosita's sputtering little engine running, so I said, "Go ahead and turn your car off and come in. I still have to put some shoes on."

Danny just stared at me, then glanced across the street to where one of my neighbors was mowing his lawn with a power mower. Then, pretending to be greatly hurt, but in a steady voice, Danny said, "My car *is* turned off."

I looked across the street and gulped. "Oh." Then I smiled. "I knew that."

Danny fumed.

"Oh, come on. Please don't be mad at me," I said, pulling him into the house.

"You think Rosita sounds like a lawn mower."

"No I don't."

"You do. Caught you red-handed."

I started laughing. Poor Danny loves his car so much that he was determined to pout, not smile, about the mix-up. "I love Rosita," I said, trying to sound sincere.

"You're lying again," he said.

"True," I admitted. "C'mon. Don't feel so bad. What do I know about engines, anyway? I hear this buzz and I figured—"

"This buzz?!" Danny was indignant, yet trying not to laugh. "Rosita *buzzes* now."

Flustered, I could tell I was only digging myself in deeper. "I love barbecue, don't you?" I said, changing the subject. "Let's go—" and I pulled him out the door. Rule of thumb: always be careful when commenting on your date's automobile. Some of these cars are alter egos.

I also went out with Ron twice more. (Not in grubbies, thank you.) He made me a delicious dinner, then we went to a movie premiere and a fun party afterwards. Ron apologized for the bowling stunt and volunteered to dress any way I ordered and go to any embarrassing place I chose. We laughed as I pretended to come up with more and more ridiculous places, then finally I told him he didn't have to do that. It's so easy to forgive someone who genuinely feels bad.

The next time, he picked me up about fifteen minutes ahead of schedule. When I asked him why, he said, "Well, last time I was late, so this time I thought I'd be early to make up for it." What a guy. Oh—and the meeting with his mom? It went great. His mom is exactly like mine. But then Ron's mission papers came through, and in just a few weeks he was off to serve a mission in Japan.

Then my friend James Olbern came back from Europe and headed right up to BYU to get some course credits before going on his mission.

"Hey, Louisa," Darin teased, "Better get a computer so you can write to all your missionaries." (How can I share a genetic link to this guy?)

Actually, I decided long ago not ever to "wait" for a missionary in the sense of not dating others. Fortunately, none of these guys could really be considered a boyfriend anyway, so writing an occasional friendly letter sounded like a fun way to keep in touch.

I kept working at the bookstore, and every week Heather, Kelly, and I would spend time together. Somehow we sensed that autumn would bring both separation and change to our friendships. Maybe one of us would go on a mission, or off to another school, or get married within a year or two—who was to say? We'd always been such close friends, and we wanted to cement those relationships while there was still time.

But we dated, too. And while many of our dates were fun, we each encountered what we started to call our Friday Night Follies— those awful dates when you wish you had just stayed home with a good book.

My experience of bowling in a formal gown kicked off the summer, but it wasn't long before Heather went on a topper. Her cousin set her up with a blind date who asked her to go deep-sea fishing. Well, this sounds like fun, particularly if you like filet of bass, which Heather does. But for Heather, bass is grown in supermarkets and is fully mature when resting in a Styrofoam tray, covered with Saran Wrap. In her life, she never pictured what it was like to bait your own hook with some slimy creature who's sure to show up in your next nightmare.

This guy was not about to let her off the hook, either. (Please. Allow me one terrible pun per book.) So Heather, choking on the odor of rotting fish slime, or whatever it is they smear all over commercial fishing boats, is slipping around on the deck, freezing to death ("Hey, I thought since it was in the ocean I should dress for the beach"), and trying to spear a slithering squid with a sharp hook.

Just as she baits the hook and throws in her line, it tangles with a most unamused fellow-fisherman beside her. The guy begins to make rude comments about girls on fishing boats and how they ought to have a novice side of the boat, and then Heather's date snags a stingray or something—I don't know, to hear Heather tell it, the thing could have been a walrus—and he reels it in. All the other guys are whooping and cheering for him, and finally he pulls it up above the surface of the water, through the air and whap! it smacks Heather right in the old kisser.

Needless to say, this was not the highlight of Heather's dating life.

Then Kelly went out with a guy who was home from school for the summer, someone she'd had a crush on since childhood. But during the date, he kept asking her strange questions. "Do you like to sew?" "Are you cheerful in the mornings?" "How much television do you watch in a week?" "Do you keep a journal and read your scriptures?"

Now Kelly, of all people, could pass such queries with flying colors; she's one of those people who excels at everything she does, and has great discipline and enthusiasm. But his line of questioning started to seem like just that—a line of questioning instead of a normal conversation. Kelly felt as if he were interviewing prospective brides and checking off a list of qualifications.

After the date, Kelly said she wished she would have said, "Wait a minute. This is a two-way street. Can you overhaul an engine? Can you rewire a kitchen or put in a sprinkler system? And what kind of priesthood leader do you plan to be? Will you share midnight feedings and diapering? Are you willing to serve in church callings? How did you do on your mission? Let's hear your testimony."

Heather and I laughed as we imagined her putting him through the same sort of exam. When you date someone and get to know them, of course you come to find out all that you need to in a natural way. But write this down: a date shouldn't feel like a job interview.

One night in July, my Aunt Melva came over to drop off Kirby, her cat. She was going on a vacation and didn't dare put Kirby in a kennel (or, more likely, there is no kennel in this town that will rent so much as an inch of space to a cat who howls every minute and a half. You could time soft-boiled eggs by this cat).

So just as she's unloading this continuous siren in our living room, she turns and says to me, "Louisa, I predict that the next boy you date will be the one you marry." (Not if he meets that cat, I thought to myself.)

"Oh, Melva," Mother blushed. "Louisa's much too young to marry."

Aunt Melva was liberated long ago from the pinching constraints of rational thought. Her eyes narrowed into slits as she scrutinized me. "Mark my words." Right about here you expect to hear lightning and see Aunt Melva disappear into a cloud of smoke *(with* her cat, hopefully), but all that happens when she makes these predictions is that Dad soon ushers her out, closes the door, and shakes his head. This time, the cat was left behind.

The next day I met a guy named Hans, who was a foreign exchange student from Sweden. He had come into the store for some books on bird watching and swept me off my feet. Here he was, towering and Nordic, with eyes like limpid pools of aquamarine. (Okay, you caught me—I've been browsing through those cheap gothic romance books.) The guy was tall and he had blue eyes—is that better?

Anyway, he had such a darling accent and he seemed so lost and so grateful for my assistance. And then, he bought a rather intellectual book about birds, which impressed me tremendously since the last guy I'd gone out with needed help unlocking his car door. And now for the capper: Hans said he'd love to know more about the Mormon Church.

Parenthetically, I have perfected at least a dozen ways to mention my religion to strangers. I have found there is always a way to work it into the conversation, just so the person knows where you stand. And guys who want to date me will know at the outset what they can expect (and not expect, if you know what I mean). In Hans's case, when he said he was from Sweden, I asked if he skied (yes!) and told him that because I'm Mormon, I often go up to Utah to ski. Ta-da. See?

So Hans asked if I had any interest in bird watching (I did now), and soon he had arranged to pick me up at 5:30 the next morning, so we could watch some native something-or-other at its most active feeding time.

Well, at 5:30 in the morning, I was in the bathroom putting mascara onto eyes that didn't even want to open yet, and my dad knocked at the door.

"Louisa," he said, "there's some fool kid in the driveway with a bullhorn and a bird whistle. He's driving Kirby crazy. I assume he's one of your friends."

I dashed to a window and stared down into the driveway. Sure enough, there was Hans in hiking boots and shorts, blowing a bird whistle into a bullhorn.

"What have I gotten myself into?" I whispered to myself, then dashed outside to keep Hans from tweeting the whole neighborhood awake. We sped away in his Volvo, and soon we were drawing blood on our legs as we scraped through stickers and bushes like a couple of hermits trying to find the least-civilized recesses of the Santa Monica Mountains.

"Isn't this far enough?" I kept asking.

"No," Hans would say and insist that I keep quiet so as not to disturb the wildlife.

Well, this is a terrific date, I thought. No talking, just walking.

Finally Hans stopped and raised his binoculars to his eyes. I stood quietly beside him for about six minutes. "What do you see?" I finally asked.

"Shh."

I waited some more. "Can I look?" I asked.

"Shh."

It went on like this for about fifteen minutes and finally I sat down on a rock. Bird watching is one thing. But bird watcher watching is past my limit.

Did you know that ants, as well as birds, get up early in the morning? I did not know this pertinent piece of information, but discovered it shortly, as ants began to bite my skin where my skin met the rock. (No wonder the birds get up early; they're after a breakfast of ants.) I leaped from my perch and yelped, slapping at my shorts and dancing around as if I were on hot coals.

Hans was furious. "You scared it away!" he shouted.

"Well pardon the ants in my pants," I said. "What am I supposed to do—sit there and let them eat me alive?"

"You could have sat somewhere else," Hans hissed. "Now the bird is gone for the day."

"What do you mean, 'gone for the day'?" I asked. "Did he hang a little sign outside his door, with clock hands pointing to the next available appointment?"

Hans didn't understand, I guess, because they don't have those sorts of signs in Sweden.

"Surely that can't be the only bird of its kind in this area," I whispered, trying to recover the feeling of scientific discovery.

But Hans could not be comforted, and we marched unceremoniously back to the Volvo. So much for Aunt Melva the Mystic.

When I got home, Mom and Dad were just getting up and making breakfast. The aroma of link sausage drew me into the kitchen where they both looked up, surprised.

"Back so soon?" Dad asked.

"Yeah." I stuck a fork into one of the sausages, then let it drain on a paper towel. "We sort of had an argument."

This was Mom's cue to offer up some worn cliché that's supposed to make it all better, but which usually just makes it all the more confusing. "Well," she said, "it takes two to tango."

"So who wants to tango?" I said.

"Oh, all right," Dad said, pretending I had tossed out an invitation. He jumped up from his chair, twirled me around, and went tangoing (tangoing?) down the hall with me. Kirby hid under the table.

I started cracking up and by the time we got back to the kitchen, I realized that my dad was probably the best date I've ever had, the most fun companion, and the best buddy in the world. He always knew how to cheer me up.

"Thanks," I said.

Dad settled right into his newspaper as if nothing had happened and said, "Don't mention it."

CHAPTER SIX
My Favorite Date

Bill and Wendy got married in late July. A couple of days before the wedding, they came over to the house for dinner, and were cooing over each other on the sofa when I got home from work.

"So. You two on drugs now?" I asked.

"Oh—hi, sis. I didn't see you come home," Bill said.

"Obviously."

"Now, Louisa, just wait until you get married," Wendy said.

"I plan to," I said, wiggling my eyebrows, "and so should *you* two." Then I grinned, watching Bill and the soon-to-be-Mrs.-Bill squirm and blush.

Mother, her radar in peak form as she sensed that I was about to launch into advice for the nearlyweds, came zooming in from the kitchen. "Louisa, could you help me in here?"

"What—these guys sat in some Crazy Glue?" I said, dog-tired after shelving the heaviest books ever published. Bill and Wendy were back in the Twilight Zone again, staring weakly into each other's eyes and sighing.

I made an instant calculation of my choices. I could go into the kitchen and help Mom do some mundane task such as peeling potatoes, or I could stay in the living room with Anthony and Cleopatra, and eventually throw up.

"You know," Mom said, as she tied an apron around me, "they're getting married in only two days. I think it's finally hit them."

No, some noxious fumes have hit them, and they're both sitting there with brain damage, unable to see anything except the dilated pupils in each other's eyes.

"Am I going to be like that?" I asked.

Mom laughed.

"Well, am I?"

Now Mom just looked at me, not sure whether I actually expected an answer or not. Finally she just shook her head, still chuckling, and pulled out some pots and pans.

The next day at work, Mr. Cooper asked me to clean the windows where little kids, whose mothers had just bought them an ice cream cone three stores down the mall, had left fingerprints. It was kind of cute, really; the fingerprints were all in front of the children's books display. Most of the marks were concentrated in front of books whose covers kids wanted to reach out and grab. One book had Big Bird on the cover, another had a blue dinosaur. From the mall side, you could hardly see the books for all the smudges.

"You know," I said, as Mr. Cooper handed me the cleaner and a rag, "you wouldn't have this problem if you'd take the kids' books out of the window."

Mr. Cooper smiled. "Kids are the perfect consumers. They see it, they want it, they grab it. Or they try to. I wish adults were the same way."

I thought about a recent date I'd had to fight off. "Some are," I mumbled. And then, before I could retract my comment, Mr. Cooper picked right up on it.

"Sounds like your social life hasn't lacked for excitement," Mr. Cooper said, laughing the way people do when they later say, "No, I was laughing *with* you, not at you" (only you weren't laughing).

I didn't want him to think I was dating a bunch of animals, so I defensively sputtered, "Yes it has!" And then, "I mean—" Then I sighed. Exasperated, I stared him straight in the eye. "You know what I mean."

"Well," he said, with a told-you-so tone, "you wouldn't have had that problem if you had let me arrange a date for you with Mark Davis. Now *there's* a gentleman."

Oh, please. Not this again. I picked up the window cleaner and headed for the door, reading the label so as to look preoccupied. Semi-odorless, it said. I rolled my eyes. What kind of company boasts such a half-success? If you can't make the thing entirely odorless, why bring it up?

I was finishing the windows just as Bill came up behind me. "Boo!"

I whipped around, startled. "Oh, Bill—hi!" He walked into the store with me, where Mr. Cooper was talking with a customer who was saying she once lived in a house owned by James Michener's secretary (which is like claiming you know Barbra Streisand's pool man, right?).

"Can I take you to lunch?" Bill asked.

"Are you serious?" I said, hoping he was. "I mean, you're getting married tomorrow. Don't you have a lot to do?"

Well, this caught the attention of not only Mr. Cooper, but his name-dropping customer who now had an even juicer tale to tell, about some hussy in the bookstore who dates a man on the very day before he marries someone else. The customer scurried off and Mr. Cooper's eyes danced with intrigue.

"Another panel member?" Mr. Cooper asked.

"Mr. Cooper," I said, determined not to get tangled in misunderstanding again, "this is my brother."

Mr. Cooper winked. "Oh, I see. I know how you Mormons are: *everybody* is your brother, right?"

Now Bill, in a moment of utter mental depletion, decided that one last practical joke played upon his baby sister prior to his wedding, couldn't really change the course of history. So instead of leaping to my rescue, Bill put his arm around me and said, "Louisa, it's all right. You can tell your boss that I'm your boyfriend."

My eyes were never wider than they were as I stared, furious, at Bill. "I will get you for this," I vowed.

Bill gave Mr. Cooper a sappy little grin and said, "Mind if I take my sweetie to lunch?"

Well this was hilarious: Mr. Cooper was actually trying to be cool. Here was a man who calls cars "sedans," admires Mark Davis, thinks wing tips go with everything, and now he was trying to look sophisticated, as if he's in the know and accepts that everybody chases around right up until their wedding day. "Sure!" he said, as if this sort of thing happens all the time.

"Mr. Cooper," I whined, "this man's sweetie is, at this moment, having her nails done for her wedding."

Now Mr. Cooper shrugged. "Listen, if it's okay with her, it's okay with me."

"But it's not okay with her," I said.

Well, this changed things. Now Mr. Cooper frowned. "I really don't think I should get involved in this triangle," he said, backing off.

I followed him. "What triangle? There is no triangle. The only triangle is the one clanging in Bill's head right now." I was mad enough to spit. "Bill!" I snarled. "If you don't tell Mr. Cooper that you're my brother, I'll—I'll—"

Now Bill was cracking up, wheezing as if his sides would split.

"This is not funny," I said, stomping my feet.

"There you go stomping again," Bill said, pointing and laughing. "She always used to do that when she was little. Like a tempest in a teapot."

I turned to my boss. "There—you see? Who but a brother would know that?"

Now Mr. Cooper took a big breath and smiled. "Go on, you two. I must say, Louisa, you keep things around here . . . *interesting.*"

On the way out, we passed the cash register where I tore off a piece of paper we had taped up a few weeks ago. I handed it to Bill.

"What's this?" he said.

"Read it," I said. "It's my new motto."

Bill turned it right side up and read aloud. "NO BILLS OVER TWENTY. Very funny."

I smiled. "I will get even with you, you know."

Bill grinned. "No you won't. By the time you think of something, I'll have thought of something else. You'll never catch up."

"Maybe not," I said. "But I'll have fun trying."

Bill swung his arm around me. "Read the back," I said. He turned the paper over and read, "Checks will be dishonored."

"Is that a dumb sign or what?" I asked. "They had that posted in the bookstore when I first started working there. How do you dishonor a check—print bowling balls on it?"

Now Bill laughed and gave me a squeeze. "I love you, Louisa. I love how your weird little mind works."

I hugged him back. "So I took down the sign and put one up that said, 'No checks.' I hope people from Czechoslovakia won't be offended."

Now Bill groaned. "You're getting worse, Louisa. Come on, here's the place," he said, pulling me into a Chinese restaurant.

"By the way, how did you find time to take your little sister to lunch on the day before your wedding?" I asked.

Bill hid behind his menu. "Well, all the arrangements are made, really. I mean, if we're not ready now, we never will be, you know? And Wendy's busy getting a facial or something, so—boy, I hope I can recognize her tomorrow."

We laughed. Then Bill lowered his menu. There were tears in his eyes. "Plus . . . I just . . . I don't know. I'm gonna miss you, Louisa."

Now, suddenly, I felt a huge lump in my throat, and I threw my arms around him.

A waiter, well-schooled in the poor timing of so many waiters, said, "So! Have you decided?" Then when he saw us both blubbering, he said, "I'll come back."

"Hey—that's the answer, Bill," I said.

"Huh?'"

"What the waiter said: 'I'll come back.' You'll just have to come back a lot, that's all. We'll still be brother and sister."

"I know. I guess I'm just afraid it will be . . . different."

I looked into Bill's face, the cheeks and chin I'd known all my life. I hoped Wendy loved all the little details about Bill the way I did. "It probably will be different," I said. "You'll have a wife. But then someday I'll have a husband, and we'll both have kids and they'll play together with their cousins. It'll just get better and better."

Bill looked at me. "I know," he whispered. "It's just that . . . It's hard to leave your family. I love Wendy; it isn't that. It's just . . . I keep thinking about the time we went tubing down that river, and I hid behind that tree and you thought I had drowned and how hard you cried. That was the first time I realized you loved me."

I punched him, teasing. "That was a dirty trick," I said. "I'm glad you reminded me. That's another one I have to get even for."

Bill laughed now and wiped his eyes with his napkin. "Do you remember that?"

I leaned against Bill's shoulder. "Yeah. I do. And the time we ate that whole lemon pie that Mom was supposed to take to the Morgan funeral." We laughed, remembering the trouble we got into for that.

"I was sure the next funeral would be a double one—ours," Bill said.

Through the whole lunch, Bill and I reminisced. Despite his being six years older than me, we had shared a lot of childhood together. Maybe we just needed to reassure each other that the memories were forever, that we would always hold each other in our hearts, never forgetting the precious times that we'd been through together. We both felt so grateful to be sealed as a family; it felt as if God had promised us the memory-making wasn't over.

"I love you, Bill," I said. "I'll still call you and stuff."

"And I'll be there for you," he promised me back. "Come marriage or high water."

Now we both laughed. "I won't tell Wendy you put it that way," I said. "Somehow I don't think she'd appreciate it."

The next day, they tied the knot. Or I guess, since they got married in the temple, I should say God tied the knot. What a difference, when you think about that. If God ties a knot, he means it to stay tied, and it's going to be tied completely differently than if a man ties the knot. You know?

I was so proud of Bill. I am so determined to be worthy to marry in the temple. I am absolutely committed to that goal, and I really look forward to the event as a glorious bonding together of myself, my husband, and Heavenly Father.

When Bill and Wendy came out of the temple, they both looked absolutely radiant. Bill kept glancing down at Wendy with the most tender expression in his eyes that I have ever seen. And Wendy would look up at him (she's a good foot shorter than he is), and it was as if her face were bathed in some kind of light beaming from Bill's eyes or something. They were basking in the glow of the love they shared—not only the love they shared for each other, but the love they each had for God and for the restored gospel. It was awesome.

The reception, except for my having to wear yellow (not my best color) went great. I looked around at Wendy's family and realized that now I'm sealed to them, too, via Bill. We were all family now. Have you ever seen two water droplets side by side, and suddenly they pull together and become one? I felt like our family had merged with Wendy's, and now we were one big droplet. (I tried to explain this to Darin, and he just made some crack about me being all wet.)

But even Darin enjoyed it and took the "you're next" teasing (which I suppose is standard for the other brother) with good humor. I almost got teary again, thinking about Darin getting married and recalling all my childhood memories with him, too. (Then I shook myself and muttered, "Wait. This is *Darin* you're talking about. Not to worry.")

Mom and Dad were beaming all over the place, Mom stopping now and then to dab her eyes with a hanky. My sister Barbara and her family stayed seated, more or less. (I told you in my last book, she has this one child who's a terror—and the kid kept bolting from the table like an emergency flare.) But Barb would grab little Megan and sit her down again fast. I still don't get why she doesn't just handcuff Megan to something (Darin, for example).

I ate with Heather, Kelly, and Lauren, Wendy's little sister. We polished off our plates of catered goodies, then watched as Bill and Wendy began dancing across the floor to a beautiful waltz. Wendy had been active in ballroom dancing at BYU and had even accomplished the nearly impossible in teaching Bill a little of it. Boy, her efforts sure paid off; I've never seen a more gorgeous couple, swirling and floating across a ballroom. Wendy chose the perfect wedding dress to dance in, too. The train wasn't too long, and the skirt was billowy and full. I half expected little fairies to zap the dress blue and then pink and then blue again, just like in the movie *Sleeping Beauty.*

As I watched them gliding along, I studied Bill's face. There he was, the guy who taught me how to throw water balloons and pitch a fast-ball. The guy who got the ticks off our dog even though it was my responsibility. The guy who helped me with homework, who let me wear his letterman's jacket to an oldies' party and didn't yell at me for wrecking it, the guy who sacrificed the best skiing days of the year so he could help his little sister on the bunny hill.

I thought about the time when I was ten and he was sixteen and he had to sing a solo in church. I'd been taking piano lessons and was going to accompany him. I'd practiced for weeks, but when the big moment came I got flustered and started hitting wrong notes. Bill knew I'd be humiliated and feel terrible, so he started singing louder and louder to drown me out. By the time the song was over, he was practically screaming.

Afterwards Bill had hurried to my side to assure me that it went all right. All I could do was laugh and cry at the same time. Laugh, because Bill had sounded so terrible, but cry, because he'd done it all for me.

And then I thought about yesterday when Bill took me out for lunch . . . how we had sat there in that Chinese restaurant and cried happy tears together, telling one another how much we love each other.

Looking back at the summer after my senior year, that hour of time with Bill stands alone with a singular golden sheen around it. Of all the dates I've had since then, I still think that lunch with Bill was truly the best date I've ever had.

CHAPTER SEVEN
I Dream of Jeannie With the Light Green Hair

Two weeks before I headed up to Utah for school, Mom and Dad sent me to New York. Wait—it's not like it sounds. They didn't exactly ship me off ("Now go to New York—and don't come back").

See, I had made friends with this girl in seminary, named Jeannie. She'd had a rough life, but was a fighter and overcame great obstacles to repent and really get her life on track. I've never seen such determination and such a turnaround. She's quite a lady and I really wanted to stay friends with someone that valiant.

Anyway, I had promised Jeannie I'd visit her on a vacation this summer, since she'd moved back East to live with an aunt and uncle in New York. My folks know I love New York City and musicals and big buildings (why wasn't I born in Manhattan?), so some time ago they promised to let me go there if I could stay with Jeannie.

We had a wonderful time. We saw the sights, ate fabulous food, and stayed up late every night, talking and giggling like two girls at a slumber party. Her aunt and uncle were so open and warm, I felt like I'd known them all my life.

They had three other kids who were sometimes well-behaved and sometimes annoying (in other words, stark-raving normal), and every Monday night they have "Family Van Evening." "We're home every single night, cooped up with each other," Uncle Barry said, rolling his eyes to exaggerate his suffering, "New York, y'know. Crime on the streets and all. So on Family Home Evening, we get the heck out of Dodge, if you know what I mean. We go bowling (not in formals, I assume), miniature golfing, out to Long Island—you name it. If it can be done in one evening, we've done it." And always they work a lesson into the travel time or around the activity.

This particular Monday they played indoor tennis at the top of some office building. Uncle Barry had a connection to the executive exercise penthouse something-or-other and got them to let kids use the courts.

You should have seen Uncle Barry. "You are watching my dream of having a kid of mine win Wimbledon . . . go right down the drain," he said to me as he chased the millionth stray ball. Jeannie is an excellent athlete, however, and it wasn't long before Uncle Barry realized that he, not I, was the appropriate tennis partner for Jeannie, and soon Aunt Lois and I were chasing balls while Jeannie and Uncle Barry were rallying the ball on the next court over. Afterwards, we went out for some kind of Italian desserts that I'd never tasted before, but wanted to be kept alive on forever.

Aunt Lois is not the greatest cook, but she didn't pretend to be. "Hey," she said, in a heavy Brooklyn accent, "when I die, nobody needs to write 'good cook' on my headstone, okay?"

"You got a deal," Uncle Barry said, then, quickly, he smiled at her.

Every night she served chicken. The first night, she just dipped the pieces in barbecue sauce and baked them. Not a bad idea, I thought. But then she let them cook so long that they overbaked and nobody could eat much. The next night, she served slices of the same leftover chicken in sandwiches.

"Yo, Lois," Uncle Barry shouted into the kitchen. "Couldn't you just put the thing out of its misery and fix hamburgers?"

A wet dishcloth landed squarely on Uncle Barry's bald head. You got the feeling Aunt Lois has lobbed a dishcloth once or twice before.

Then on the third night, she tore up the remaining leftover chicken and tossed it into a green salad. Uncle Barry stuck his fork in and pulled out a hard, stringy piece. "What is this—the Chicken from Hell? It keeps coming back!"

By now all of us were in hysterics and even Aunt Lois was laughing. "One little lie. I tell one little lie and I have to pay for it the rest of my life."

"What lie?" Jeannie asked.

"When we were dating, I told Barry I could cook. A slight exaggeration."

Now Uncle Barry was poking through his salad as if for bodies. "Slight exaggeration? A bigger lie never fell from the lips of mankind."

Aunt Lois plopped down beside him and leaned in for him to hug her, which he did with a naturalness that told me they were very affectionate with each other. "Oh, Barry," she said. "You love me anyway."

"Sad, but true," he said. And then, teasing Jeannie and me, "Don't you let me catch you false advertising to *your* dates."

Now Aunt Lois pretended to be stunned. "But of course they will," she said. "That's what we're learning at Relief Society's Mother-Daughter night tomorrow."

Aunt Lois was the Relief Society president and had a big makeover evening of cosmetics and fashions planned. As Uncle Barry eyed her suspiciously, she bubbled over with laughter. "Wanna come?"

Uncle Barry kept poking his greens. "I'll have no part of an evening that teaches women to say they can cook when they can't. Ah—a radish. I'm rich!" Uncle Barry popped the radish into his mouth, acting as if it were a moist delicacy.

The next night Jeannie and I sat with all the other girls and their moms, listening to experts tell us how to apply make-up and what clothes flatter which figures.

One woman in the class shared a remarkable trick. "If you're out of red lipstick," she said, as if about to reveal a great mystery, "you can use dampened red felt." Well, it's hard to imagine being clean out of even the oldest of your lipsticks, and yet be brimming with a fresh supply of crimson felt. However, assuming you have found yourself in this most unusual of circumstances, one must then wonder how such a marvel is to be applied, and if it's with the fingers, then do you wear gloves to conceal the red fingertips which must surely result, or just keep your hands in your pockets all evening?

A sewing expert then showed us how to fashion a skirt entirely from men's neckties. By sewing enough of them together vertically, you can eventually surround your lower half with a limitless series of stripes and patterns that will dazzle and amaze your friends. She didn't say how to gather together enough ties to cover one's equator, but it was plain to see that no one but a curmudgeon would refuse to hand over his entire collection of neckties, once this wise purpose is explained to him.

At this point, Jeannie whispered, "Let's split," but I persuaded her to stay for the next mini-class, which promised to be a little more enlightening. It was on being datable, and was taught by the elders quorum president and his wife. Now we were getting somewhere. They talked about being the kind of girl a guy wants to ask out in the first place.

Someone who makes others feel accepted and good about themselves. They said it was important to be interested in others, involved in activities where you can meet various guys, and to have a happy outlook, an optimism that sees the bright side of life. They said girls should be relaxed and curious, and develop a genuine caring about others, so guys would feel free to share their thoughts with someone who truly understands.

"Remember," said the husband, "when a man is looking for a wife, he wants someone who'll be a good mother, who can manage her finances, who values education, who has great spirituality—"

"Stop," his wife teased. "You're describing the perfect woman again."

Her husband smiled. "Well, women do the same thing: they look for a man who has it all. And it's hard not to. You get a shopping list going, and it's tempting to just keep adding traits to it."

"But it's dangerous," said his wife. "I mean, you should have high standards, definitely. But some people have such extremely high expectations that nobody can meet them. We have to allow room for growth. If you wait for someone perfect, you're waiting for the Second Coming, right?" We all laughed.

"Wait a minute," teased her husband, puffing out his chest. "There are one or two perfect catches left, you know."

His wife gave him a glance. "Where?" she deadpanned. Then they talked about physical appearance. After the lessons on make-up and wardrobe, I was glad that they both put it in perspective. "It's important to know about grooming, and to look your best," said the wife, "but never substitute outer beauty for the inner qualities that matter more."

Her husband agreed. "When you go to college, watch to see who the most popular girls are. I'll bet you they'll be attractive to a certain degree, but not necessarily knockouts. Personality is a million times more important."

"On the other hand," said his wife, "there are a lot of girls who could change their life if they changed their look. I mean, just little things, like a new hairstyle. Some girls really think they don't have to do anything to enhance their appearance. And I think everybody should put forth a little effort."

"That's true," said one of the women there. "I know my husband appreciates it when I try to keep my weight down, or I fix myself up a little for him. But *I'm* the one who benefits most. I feel good about myself when I take time to look my best."

I glanced over at Jeannie, who seemed to be in deep concentration. "What are you thinking about?" I whispered. (Incidentally, most guys hate to hear this question.)

"I've got an idea," she said.

That night, Jeannie pulled me into the bathroom, then stared into the mirror. "Do me," she said.

"I beg your pardon?"

"Give me a makeover. Head to foot." She turned and whispered to me, since the littler kids were in bed across the hall. "Louisa, do you realize that I have never had one date?"

I blinked, stunned. I'd never even thought about it before. I guess Jeannie wasn't what you'd call a gorgeous specimen of femininity. But not being a guy, I'd never thought twice about whether she was attractive in that way; she was my buddy and all I knew was that we'd had great fun together.

"I mean it," Jeannie said. "I want to look good. I want to be pretty. You think I could?"

"Jeannie, I think you misunderstood tonight. Guys ask you out because of your personality. That's what makes a girl popular."

Jeannie smiled. She's one sharp cookie. "Yeah, but if they aren't drawn to your looks at least a little bit, they're never going to find out whether you have a good personality or not."

"Well . . . ?"

"Louisa, I'm not trying to be phony; I just want a new look. What do you say?"

I stared at her features a different way, now. I imagined her with make-up, her hair fluffed up a little, a pair of earrings. I grinned, excited. "Okay—I'll get my stuff."

We stayed up until midnight contouring, shading, highlighting and trying on various shades of lipstick. Jeannie practiced doing it herself and borrowed my curling iron.

The next morning everybody was eating breakfast except Jeannie, who hadn't come out of the bathroom for thirty minutes.

"Is Jeannie all right?" asked Aunt Lois. "She's not sick or anything is she?"

"Uh, no, I don't think so," I said, slathering cream cheese onto my bagel. I had completely forgotten about last night.

Suddenly the door opened and in walked Christie Brinkley. Or at least a close facsimile. Every person's jaw dropped open! Jeannie just stood there, blushing.

"Wow! Jeannie looks like a princess," said one of the tiny kids.

Uncle Barry looked like an unwrapped mummy. He was frozen stiff, with a bagel half-way to his open mouth. His eyes didn't even blink.

Aunt Lois was the first to move, and she stood up, pulling out a chair for Jeannie. "Your Highness," she said, curtsying low.

Now Jeannie laughed. Even her *laugh* seemed different. I couldn't help staring. Jeannie nudged me with her elbow. "Knock it off, will you?" she said. "I don't look that different."

"Are you kidding?" I mumbled. "I thought you were a burglar."

Jeannie laughed. "Come on, everybody. You can eat now."

The kids went back to their Cap'n Crunch, but Uncle Barry just kept staring. Finally he turned to Aunt Lois. "Did they do this to all the women in the ward? If so, I'm not going to recognize a single person at church Sunday."

Aunt Lois winked at Jeannie. "I think this is something Jeannie and Louisa cooked up afterwards."

Jeannie smiled, really proud of herself. Her whole demeanor seemed . . . I don't know . . . suddenly elegant or something. Uncle Barry shook his head, "Well, the end of an era," he said.

"The what?" Jeannie asked.

"The end of the era of peace and quiet around here. Before you know it, every kid and his brother will be knocking on the door and calling on the phone." He sighed, doing his put-upon act again. Then, all of a sudden, he brightened.

"Hey—this means I get to check out the dates! All right!" He was practically rolling up his sleeves in happy anticipation of being the interrogator.

Jeannie cast me a forlorn look. "I'm in for it," she sighed.

I bit into my bagel. "Yup."

That afternoon we went shopping. Jeannie was excited over her new look and wanted some more feminine clothes to go with it. I felt like I was taking somebody shopping who had just landed from another planet.

"What do you wear these with?" she asked, picking up a pair of earrings and a matching pin.

"A jacket like that," I said, pointing across the store. "And this scarf." I tied a red silk scarf around her neck.

"Hey," she said, "how'd you do that?"

On the way home, Jeannie got carried away and bought some hair dye. "I'm going lighter," she said.

"What?!"

"Why not? If it looks awful, I'll dye it back again."

"Jeannie, are you sure you want to do this?" I was uneasy and began to wonder if I was a good influence.

But there was no stopping her now. She wasn't even reading the label—she just grabbed a platinum blonde color and headed for the check-out counter.

"You're out of control," I said. "I'm calling Looks-Anon."

Jeannie just laughed. That afternoon while Aunt Lois took the kids out, Jeannie mixed the dye in a squeeze bottle and squirted it on. "I think you've gone over the deep end," I said.

"Yeah, but if I look great, you're going to do the same thing, right?"

"Of course," I said, and shrugged. Why quarrel with success?

A timer went off and Jeannie stepped into the shower to wash it out. I settled down with one of the fashion magazines she'd bought along with the dye at the drugstore.

In ten minutes, Jeannie dashed out in a robe, with a towel on her hair. Her eyes were as round as this morning's bagels.

"What happened?" I asked, following her back into the bathroom.

"It's green," Jeannie whispered. "Light green."

"Oh, don't be ridiculous," I said. "Hair never goes green. Here. Take the towel off and let's dry it."

Slowly Jeannie unwrapped her turban. And there it was: greenish, ash-blonde hair. I gasped. Jeannie's eyes welled with tears as she stared at herself in the mirror. The gorgeous girl of the morning had turned into a real-life space alien.

"What am I going to do?" she asked, her voice trembling. Just then Uncle Barry came home.

"Hello," he called. "Don't everybody rush to greet me at once."

"Hi—we're in the bathroom," I called out.

"Shh," Jeannie said. "I can't let anyone find out." She began wrapping her hair in the towel again.

"Well, we can't just hide in here," I said.

Suddenly Uncle Barry was in the doorway. "Oh—a friend of mine wanted to meet you, Jeannie." We could both tell from his tone that he had wasted no time whatsoever spreading word that his niece was now drop-dead gorgeous, and this "friend" was a guy who might want to ask her out.

Jeannie's eyes darted from side to side as she tried to think of an excuse. "Well, I just washed my hair. I—I'm not really presentable. Could he come back—tomorrow?"

"Hey, no problem," Uncle Barry said. "He wants to see my stamp collection anyway. We'll just wait for you to dry it." And suddenly he had disappeared back into the living room.

"Now what?" Jeannie hissed, as if I had gotten her into this. After a few minutes of frantic whispering, we decided Jeannie would sneak down the hall, get dressed, then we'd both climb out a window and dash to the nearest salon to have the green taken out.

But just as the two of us landed on the ground below, the front door opened and out came Uncle Barry with his "friend," an incredibly handsome guy who looked about twenty-three and had a gleaming Jaguar parked at the curb. They had come outside so Uncle Barry could show the guy the mealy bugs (or whatever they were) that were eating his trees.

Uncle Barry just stared at us. There I was, shaking and trembling and looking like the Bad Influence Chick from California, and there was Jeannie, fresh out of the shower with no make-up on, red eyes from crying, and hair that any punk rocker would be proud to own.

"Jeannie! What happened to you?" Uncle Barry was aghast.

Jeannie looked at me. "Well, um . . ."

I shrugged. Heck if *I* knew anything about this—I'm just the Avon lady, right?

Uncle Barry's friend simply stared. Finally he came over and shook our hands. Oh, great, I thought. Looks, money, botanical expertise, and now manners, too. Jeannie was blowing it with a good catch. Jeannie was turning pale, as if she might faint. Or maybe it was the contrast of green against her skin.

"Uncle Barry," I said, "we were on our way to fix this. It was an accident."

"That's right," Jeannie said, as if it weren't. "That's exactly what we were going to do."

Uncle Barry's friend soon angled toward his car, and after muttering some feeble line about the late hour, he peeled out of there. Uncle Barry just stood there, red-faced and suspicious. Were we lying? Were we secretly chemists who used our heads as stir sticks?

"What is this," he finally asked, "another Relief Society mini-class run amok?"

Jeannie began to cry and explained the whole thing. "I just got so excited because I . . . I never felt pretty before today."

Now Uncle Barry just stared at his feet. He pulled her to him and hugged her. "Oh, Jeannie," he whispered. "You have always been beautiful. You just didn't know it."

Jeannie looked up at her uncle. "You really mean that, don't you?"

Uncle Barry nodded, then touched her green hair and smiled. "Even with green hair," he said.

Now Jeannie laughed. "This is the worst I have ever looked in my life, huh?" We all joined in now, the timing of Uncle Barry's friend giving us the biggest laugh of all.

Just then Aunt Lois came home with the children. The kids ran up to Jeannie and twirled her around in a giant embrace. One little boy noticed her hair and happily squealed, "Gross! Disgusting! Can I paint my hair green, too?"

"Sure," said Uncle Barry. "We'll *all* paint our hair green." The kids ran cheering into the house, leaving a bewildered Aunt Lois outside with us.

"What the heck," said Uncle Barry. "It beats teaching them tennis."

CHAPTER EIGHT

Have I Got a Guy for You

See the title of this chapter? The next time somebody comes up to you and says this line, you should pretend it is a question and say, "Probably not, but thanks anyway."

After I went up to BYU that fall, I must have had eight people say this to me, and all of them were wrong. And I, unwitting fool that I was, couldn't just let history teach me; I had to go out with every blind date and "fix-up" because I'm so blasted curious. (I hate that about me; I've been curious ever since I was a kid. While it made for great grades in science, it has made for a number of miserable social encounters.)

I got an apartment with four other girls and each of them had some guy in some class who they thought would be perfect for me. (I missed an obvious clue here: if these guys were so terrific, why didn't my roommates date them?)

And then I made a few other friends who got the same idea. What was with these people? Were they enrolled in Dating 101 and their final exam was to play Cupid with Louisa Barker?

Still, I couldn't resist. Odds alone told me that at least *one* of these dates would pan out. Who could tell, I reasoned: if I say no, maybe I'll miss the one and only true love I was predestined to meet in this life.

Let me tell you the most important thing I learned in my first year of dating at BYU: that the above paragraph is LOADED with baloney.

First of all, of course I could have resisted. I'm not some hopelessly unmarriageable maiden who has to jump at every opportunity that comes along. I'm a neat girl with a lot going for me. At least, I've worked hard on myself and I think a guy would be lucky to date me. I don't mean that in a conceited way; it's just that we should all have healthy self-opinions. My head isn't overblown and out of whack; believe me, I'm acutely aware of my weaknesses, too. But I think I'm fun, level-headed, good-hearted, committed to the gospel, and that I could bring a lot to a relationship, that's all.

Second, there *are* no odds when it comes to dating. There are no scientific laws that govern the peculiar world of the blind date, and there are no guarantees whatsoever that one will work out. I know, I know. You have two friends and a cousin who met and married Mr. Right after meeting him on a blind date. Wonderful. We should all be so lucky.

Third, my worry that I'll miss the exact right guy by turning down a blind date is ridiculous. For one thing, there are several people with whom you can be exquisitely happy, not just one lone soul searching the globe for you.

And for heaven's sake—this isn't governed by the stars or something. It isn't as if every step you take is guiding your path to intersect with some guy. What if you scoot through a yellow light and had you only waited, Mr. Right would have pulled up next to you? Or what if you get on the wrong elevator and the next one to open would have been his? Pretty silly, huh?

If you're living righteously and staying in touch with the Holy Ghost so that you truly know his voice and hear his promptings, you don't have to worry at all. When the time comes to choose your Eternal Companion, you'll have clear, unmistakable guidance and distinct answers to your prayers. That's really the key to this "but who will I marry?" dilemma.

Still, it took me eight terrible dates to gain this wisdom. (See? And all you had to do was buy one book!) Had it not been for the wholesome, fun, and terrific guys I dated in between the awful ones, I might have given up on dating altogether. The first guy I got set up with was a deeply serious fellow who asked me if I would mind being married to a prophet.

"Of course not," I said.

He smiled confidently. "Oh. That's good."

A cold tingle ran down my spine. This guy really means it! Yikes! Now, you'd think at this point I would call it quits on dating guys I'd never even met, wouldn't you?

Then there are the guys who think they've had personal revelation that you're the girl they should marry. This gives me the creeps, frankly. At first I was flattered (though I knew the guy was dead wrong), but after a few more fellows made similar comments, I grew alarmed. What kind of testimonies did these guys have if they couldn't tell real revelation from obsessive infatuation? And how many girls had they said it to?

I'm not saying that everyone who has ever made such a claim is wrong. I imagine there have been numerous cases where the still small voice has given specific direction. But those times aren't *this* numerous!

One time I got set up with a girl's cousin, who announced halfway through the date that he was a confirmed atheist. I smiled. "That's nice," I said. "Who confirmed you?"

Then I went out with a guy who had been marketed as "a diamond in the rough." He kept talking about "the ranch" he was planning to own someday. I figured he was going to raise cattle or something. A few well-placed questions later I discovered that this ranch was where he would develop a hybrid animal by breeding weasels with opossums. When I found that he knew less about biology than I knew about ranching, I figured I was dating a mad scientist who simply had an outdoor laboratory.

Listen. Just because something is in the rough does not necessarily mean it's a diamond. (There ought to be a telethon for guys like this.)

One guy had been billed as a gospel doctrine teacher in another ward, so I figured he would at least be able to speak in complete sentences. And I have to admit he was cute and funny. But after our date he wanted much more than a handshake, let me tell you. I'm lucky I scrambled out of his car with my coat still on. "What do you teach on Sundays, anyway?" I asked him. "Gospel *Lite?*"

Another time I doubled-dated with a girl whose date was just back from a mission to Italy (where James Olbern went—what did I tell you?), but from listening to him, you wouldn't even know he was LDS. Maybe he thought he sounded sophisticated or something, but his words were peppered with such foul language I could hardly endure the evening. Finally I spoke up. "You know," I said, as gently as I could, "I'd appreciate it if you could keep from swearing." (My date, who should have been the one to speak up, sat there like a nervous worm in conversation with a robin. *His* problem, I decided.)

The guy simply laughed. "Are you kidding?" he said. "Boy, you need to do some travelling. Get out and hear the way they talk in other countries."

And in which country do they speak vulgarian? Speaking of travel, this guy was going nowhere fast. At the end of the evening we dropped him off at my friend's apartment, where he hopped into his brand new "Z" and sped off. Two weeks ago he couldn't spell Z, I thought. And now he's got one.

Well, some dates are pitted and some are just the pits, eh? My date hadn't been much better. At every turn, he was pinching pennies. First, he insisted we go to the movie before having dinner, so we could get the early-bird discount. Then he tried to talk us all into a cheaper restaurant, and finally when the waiter asked us if we'd like dessert, my date quickly spoke for all of us and said no. When the check came, he gladly let Mr. Italy pick up the tab. As we were walking out, he nudged me, proud of himself. "See how I stuck him with the check?" he chortled.

You know, I can see being thrifty. I can see being frugal. In a lot of ways, it's fun to get a good bargain and even make a game out of it. But being a tightwad is inexcusable. It embarrasses those around you, particularly if you do it with such a sense of one-upmanship. This guy was not poor, either. He was simply cheap. If you're going to take someone out on a date, be prepared to spend what the date costs—or do something else you *are* willing to pay for.

Really, dates don't have to be expensive. Going for a long walk can be a terrific date. But if a guy is never willing to splurge and treat his date to a special evening, he's as wrong as the fellow who thinks every date has to be an MGM production.

Not all of my terrible dates that year were the result of blind dating. I made a few mistakes with my eyes wide open, too. I met Craig Rudman at a devotional that was so inspiring and wonderful, it left me a little goofy; I would have dated a Golden Retriever at exactly that moment and found in my new friend a number of sterling attributes.

I don't know exactly how it happened. I was just feeling so benevolent, so filled with love for the entire student body, that I forgot to be a teensy bit discriminating in my date selection. I had a dreamy smile on my face as I left the building, and I bumped smack into Craig.

Well, Craig wasted no time in assuming this was a sign from heaven that we should go out Friday night, and before I knew the first thing about him, I said yes.

Now some might say that Craig had only one oar in the water, but in fact, he had no oars. Only a pair of drumsticks. I'll explain. After two dates with Craig (they were actually pretty fun—we went to a ballgame and a dance), he instantly became possessive. Not just possessive, but insanely jealous. He forbade me to eat on campus where other guys might see me. He showed up with eerie precision after each of my classes, to walk me to the next one. He called at night and again in the morning.

Well, no shrinking violet, I raised immediate objections to this sudden smothering and told him we were through. That night I was awakened by two roommates shaking me and demanding that I get Craig out of the parking lot. I looked down out of our apartment window to the cars below, and there was Craig with a drum set and amplifiers, serenading me.

"It's the middle of the night," I croaked, my voice crackly and my eyes bleary. "What is he *doing?*"

My roommates, their hands on their hips, just smirked, "Don't ask us. He's *your* boyfriend."

I pulled on a coat and some winter boots. "Gimme a break," I said. "Two dates do not a boyfriend make. How was I to know he was psychotic?"

I hurried out into the parking lot. "Craig," I said, "what's going on?"

Craig had no clue that his musical talent was not appreciated just now. "Like it?" he said. "It's for you."

Ah. Thanks a lot. I suddenly pictured Craig with Hans, forming an oompah band. Craig could be the percussion and Hans could blow his bird whistle into that bullhorn.

"It's two in the morning," I said, sharing a little factoid that Craig had obviously overlooked.

Craig stopped drumming. "So?"

"So we're trying to sleep. Craig, listen. You and I are not dating anymore. I'm sorry."

Craig started up on the drums again, as if a different number might change my mind. I shook my head and thought, what do I do—call the police? I finally called my bishop, who came right over and had a long talk with Craig. I don't know what he said, but I do know that the cherry chocolate cheesecake I made for the bishop was the least I could do to thank him for ending that relationship pronto.

And my roommates didn't fare much better. Leslie fell head over heels in love with a guy named Alma, who asked her to marry him, then turned right around and said he thought maybe he should date some other girls first. She was crushed.

"I think I still want to marry you," he said, "but I need to be sure." Alma had been engaged twice before and had a pattern of keeping two or three girls on the hook at one time.

Well, poor Leslie was a wreck. She didn't know whether to start dating others or wait for Alma. She was afraid he'd get mad if she began dating, then she'd lose him and spend the rest of her life regretting it.

Oh, dear. Another self-esteem case. Having been there, I recognized it right away. "He should be worried that *you're* mad at *him,*" I said. "And well you should be. How can there be a double standard, Leslie? How can he just put you on hold like that while he goes off to play? Go out with someone else. I'd do it in a second. This guy is jerking you around. Alma the Yutz."

"But that's playing games," she protested.

"It is not. It's saying, 'Fine. You're not ready to make a commitment, and I'm sad because you were really the one I wanted to marry. However, I'm not going to cry in my lap for the rest of my life; I'm going to begin the search all over again.' There's nothing gamey about that. It's sincere. Or it ought to be. Sure it hurts, but what choice do you have?"

For the next six weeks, this went on: Leslie whining and ambivalent, Alma getting her hopes up and then kissing some co-ed in the hallways. Finally Leslie went out with a football player named Kirk. And this time she *really* fell in love. When Alma called to complain, Leslie was so wild about her new romance that she actually hung up on him.

I gave her a thumbs-up.

Then Sarah had a guy over for dinner, whom she claimed to have met in a history class, but who I suspect actually met her in a guns and ammunition shop. All Steve could do was talk about hunting and how stupid anyone is who opposes it. Now, look. I'm not going to get into a big debate about hunting, where I decry its bloodthirsty sport element and you then list all the Church leaders you've known who went deer hunting with your uncle. This is my book and I'll decide whose views win out on these pages.

Anyway, I suppose it goes without saying that Steve and I did not exactly hit it off. I told him that when Joseph Smith camped near a river with some companions once, he kept them from even killing a snake, saying that the serpent can never lose its venom while the servants of God possess the same disposition to destroy animals. He made the brethren carry the serpents across the creek on sticks and told them not to kill a creature of any kind during their journey.

"Yeah, but was he speaking as a prophet then, or just a camper?" Steve asked.

"Steve," I said with a sigh, "your lights are on but your plates are sealed."

Then Carla dated a fast-talking, finger-snapping bundle of energy named Mick, who burst into a room like a torpedo and immediately started telling all of us what to do.

"Who died and made *him* king?" whispered Emily.

Mick was hovering over Sarah, correcting an essay she was writing, and at the same time telling Carla exactly what to wear for their date tonight, for which she had better get dressed fast, he said. You take one look at a guy like that and you just know he drives like a maniac.

In all fairness, I've seen girls be just as impossible as guys. (And, okay, I guess my own idiosyncrasies have unnerved a fellow or two.) I've seen girls bake trunkloads of brownies and deliver half a dozen batches to all their suitors, pretending each guy is the sole recipient of their affections. I watched one girl plan elaborate hikes that "just happen" to end in a soft meadow where she earlier stashed a picnic basket, a blanket, and the most amorous intentions ever imagined. Her unwitting date was lured right into the trap like a fly into a spider web.

I've seen girls swear, drink, and make lewd advances—maybe as often as I've seen guys do it. Girls, too, can be jealous, crazy, manipulative, greedy in their collection of proposals, tight with their money, careless with the hearts they've gathered, afraid to make a commitment, and quick to judge a fellow before they've given him a chance.

I sat behind some girls in a religion class once (another of life's ironies) and thought they were discussing Nephites and Lamanites. As their voices grew louder, I realized they had categorized their dates into two groups of hunks and lemons: they called them "Beefites" and "Lemonites." They reminded me of the guys who hung out of their dorm windows with Olympic-style number cards, rating the various girls who'd walk by. Both camps are gravely in the wrong.

It's sad, if you really think about it, to realize that some people—maybe thinking it's funny—are being so thoughtless toward Heavenly Father's other children. Now granted, the only way to deal with Crazy Craig was to call my bishop. But in most cases, we need to show more sensitivity and caring for each other. It's actually a very vicious person who tries to make their partner jealous or who tries to "trick" someone into dating them. None of these ploys and machinations is in keeping with the teachings of the Church. Our bishop's wife says that mutual respect and a mature approach are what will help you not only have a happy dating life, but a happy marriage someday.

I'm so glad that most Mormon kids understand this. I've spent quite a few pages telling about some of the exceptions—the disaster dates and the girls and guys you want to run away from, screaming. But the vast majority of students I've met at BYU have been wonderful; you could almost marry any one of them and end up blissfully happy. They really are that terrific. Most of them study hard, keep their testimonies growing, and seem to have been raised with a beautiful outlook toward life and marriage.

I met a guy exactly like that, right at the beginning of my sophomore year.

CHAPTER NINE

Hearts and Whispers

His name was Joel Barnett, and I met him because the student phone directory transposed our telephone numbers. He got a call from my dad, who was—to say the least—relatively alarmed to hear a man's voice answering what he thought was his daughter's phone. They got to talking and soon laughing, and Dad told him to look me up.

Meanwhile Dad reached me (by dialing Joel's number) and told me he'd just spoken to a charming, witty, thoroughly likable prospective seminary teacher.

"I'm sure he is," I said, "but I have a new policy: no."

"No? Why not?"

I briefly explained that after having learned the hard way, I was only going to date guys after meeting them in person. Dad said that sounded reasonable.

The next Sunday while I was sitting in sacrament meeting, a rugged-looking guy in a gorgeous suit (okay, I am *trying* not to notice the clothes) slipped in and sat beside me. I know this sounds absurd, but he looked like a movie star or something. Every masculine feature on his face appeared to have been chiseled by an artist. It literally took my breath away.

"Hi," he whispered. "I'm Joel Barnett."

And I'm in love, I thought to myself. Somehow I found my tongue and mumbled "Louisa Barker," which turned out to be something he already knew, because Dad had called him back, gotten his address, and sent him a picture of me. (You know your love life is lagging when your own father has to set up something long distance.)

The meeting started and Joel opened the hymnbook, holding it out so we could share it. When I touched the cover, I thought, Oh, terrific. Now my hands are sweaty, and they're leaving little wet fingerprints on the book. Joel will think he's sitting next to a squid.

Every time I glanced up at Joel during the meeting, he smiled the most gorgeous white smile I've ever seen. I wish Heather or Kelly could have been there to slap me and keep me from staring. (Both of them went to Ricks College, by the way, where they each promptly found boyfriends and were spared the outrageous experiences I described in the last chapter.)

When sacrament meeting was over, Joel walked me home. With him beside me, I felt I could walk to Wyoming. He was dazzling and my head was thoroughly spinning.

I hummed and twirled through the apartment all evening. My roommates just shook their heads. "She's a goner," Sarah said.

I smiled; nothing could ruffle me. I had found the man of my dreams. In fact, I had always thought it sounded wonderful to be married to a man as well-versed in the gospel as seminary teachers seemed to be. They often became university Institute directors—a romantic position to hold, in my mind. I tried not to get carried away fantasizing about a fellow I had barely met, but I couldn't help imagining us having spiritual discussions late into the evening, about the Book of Revelation and the powerful lessons taught within the pages of the Book of Mormon. It was like living in the celestial kingdom here on earth, right? By the time I fell into bed, I had picked names for all of our children and planned the parties to celebrate their various graduations from seminary.

I dated Joel for the next five months. He'd been on a mission to Bolivia and spoke meltingly fluent Spanish. (Oh, what do I know? I don't speak Spanish—even Joel reading a grocery list would have melted me.) Every time I was around him, I felt lighter than air.

We studied together, made ice cream together, went shopping together and of course, went on dates every week. At the outset, we agreed to see others as well, and though I continued to date once in a while, my heart wasn't in it. Whenever I was out with someone else, all I thought about was Joel. And best of all, he seemed to feel the same way.

"So when are you two getting engaged?" Leslie asked me one morning. By now she and Kirk had already set a date and ordered the wedding dress.

I almost choked on my orange juice. "What?"

"Come on. You've been dating for months."

I smiled. "Leslie," I said, "sometimes people date for a lot longer than this before they get engaged."

Leslie leaned in and whispered, "But if he asked you, wouldn't you say yes?"

I laughed to avoid the question. "I'd have to think about it," I said. "Didn't you?"

Leslie shook her head. "Nope. I knew Kirk was the one the minute I met him." Oh, great. Another one of *those*.

Suddenly I realized that in my entire relationship with Joel, I had never prayed about whether we should marry. We had just seemed to hit it off so well that it seemed unnecessary; why pray about something so obvious? Besides, it was premature, I reasoned. Joel hadn't even approached the subject.

And frankly, I had never imagined myself being a wife this young. My goals had always included temple marriage, but that seemed to follow graduation from college, and maybe even an advanced degree or two. I knew I could still continue my schooling if I should marry, but was I through being a kid and ready to settle down? I hadn't even decided whether or not to serve a mission; how could I already be thinking of marriage? I shook these thoughts to the back corners of my mind and hurried off to meet Joel. We always walked to our first class together.

But today was to be different. When I reached Joel at the corner, instead of greeting me with a kiss on the cheek, he stood stiffly away from me, holding his books across his chest.

"Louisa, we have to talk," he said.

"What's the matter?"

"I want to break up."

I felt as if I were falling backwards down into a deep well that just spiraled on and on into the center of the earth. Everything started happening in slow motion, as if it were all on film and I was having to watch every painful frame at slow speed. This can't be happening, I thought. This must be a nightmare.

But Joel was serious. He had fallen in love with one of the other girls he'd been dating. It was as simple as that.

"I really didn't want to hurt you," Joel said. "I'm really sorry, Louisa."

I felt numb, as if someone had taken my heart and torn it into tiny pieces. My whole world seemed to shatter before my eyes. How ironic that just this morning Leslie had asked me about marrying him.

"I hope you're not angry," Joel said.

Everything he said seemed to filter through a thick buzz around the two of us. I was so hurt I couldn't stop the tears from streaming down my face.

"Please don't cry," Joel said. Was I going crazy? Would I never recover from this? Would I have to live in a padded cell for the rest of my life?

Joel sighed. "Please say something, Louisa."

Part of me still couldn't believe it. "Are you sure?" I asked.

Then he told me he had already proposed to the girl.

"You mean you waited until she said yes before cutting me loose?" I had never felt so dangled in my life. What a spineless coward, I thought. Had the girl turned him down, I suppose I would have been second choice. Suddenly I was furious.

"How dare you lead me on while you're waiting to see how things go in another relationship!" I yelled. "You talk about integrity but you don't know the meaning of the word!"

Joel was glancing around now, aware that passersby were staring. "Louisa, I said I was sorry." He tried to steer me away from the corner and down a less-populated street.

I shoved his arm away from me and shouted to him as I headed off, "Don't apologize to me," I said. "You did me a favor, buddy. You saved me from wasting any more time on a complete jerk. I feel sorry for you, Joel. And for her."

By now the lump in my throat had made it impossible to speak, and I ran the rest of the way to class, sobbing and gasping for air. I darted into the ladies' room and cried into the sink for ten minutes, splashing my face with water and trying to compose myself.

I took a few deep breaths, then sat on a little sofa in the lounge area to rest. It felt as if two little people were arguing inside my head.

One of them was a spectacled little professor, spouting all the intellectual lines: "What Joel did was a cheap trick, and you really *are* better off without him. You just spent five months in the school of hard knocks, and you graduated with honors. Someone that duplicitous would be a terrible father. You were only infatuated, anyway."

But then another little voice—that of a hysterical, frizzy-haired poet—was screaming: "Who are you kidding? Your heart is crushed to smithereens, and you'll never get over this! You'll go to your grave with Joel's name on your lips. You loved him more than any woman ever loved any man, and you may as well lie down and die."

I thought back to my conversation with Leslie, and suddenly I recalled my thought that I hadn't yet prayed about Joel. I decided to do it right now. Since classes had started, the restroom was empty, and that made it easy to kneel at the little sofa and open my heart up to Heavenly Father. I told Him exactly how I felt and asked Him to please tell me what to do and what to feel.

After praying, I decided to skip my next class and just walk. I circled the building and then headed across the lawn. All the while I kept reaching out to my Heavenly Father, reminding myself how lucky—how very lucky—I am to have such a strong testimony and marveling at the strength God must have given me, or I wouldn't be coping with this loss at all.

And then just as I reached the road, I felt as if someone had whispered these words into my mind: "He wasn't the one." All at once, in a flood of emotion, I began to cry. Only this time they were tears of joy—and relief. The Comforter had put His arms around me and spoken the plainest of truths, a simple thought that I could have heard long ago (and spared myself all this heartache), had I only thought to pray about Joel sooner.

Not only did it gladden my heart to know that Joel was not a good match for me, but I felt incredibly warm and elated inside to think that God loved me so much. Along with the answer to my prayer, I received such a strong conviction that He cares personally about each one of us and every one of our disappointments. I'd known it before, but this sort of sealed it to my soul or something. Never again could I doubt that God loved me—or any other individual. And I was humbled to realize that even though I should have asked the Lord about Joel sooner, He didn't remind me of that over-sight. He simply responded with love when I finally did reach out to him. The answer had been there all along, just waiting for me to ask for it. What a lesson! What an example of perfect parenting. I prayed again, this time offering up a prayer of thankful joy, praising my Father in Heaven and expressing unspeakable gratitude at being His daughter and being so loved by Him.

From then on, I decided not to "lean unto my own under-standing," but to approach things in partnership with God. Since then, I've had equally distinct answers to my prayers on a number of occasions, and I even read once that unless you are having spiritual experiences on a regular basis, your testimony is not growing. I'm so grateful to have learned this while I'm so young. After tasting what it feels like to "commune with the Father," I never want to lose that feeling again.

CHAPTER TEN

Pushing the Pause Button

Do you think Russell is cute?" Sarah was lying on her stomach, her knees bent and her ankles crossed as she thumbed through a magazine, slowing down when she came to the moisturizer ads.

"Oh, no you don't," I said. "I'm not walking into *that* trap again."

"What trap?"

I sighed and put down the book I was reading. "Three weeks ago Leslie asked me if I thought Kirk was good-looking. Well it just happens that he's not my type. But so what? I figured as long as Leslie thinks he's cute, that's all that should matter."

"You told her that?"

"No, I lied. I thought I'd be polite and I told her that yes, I think he's good-looking. So for a whole week, Leslie wouldn't speak to me, because she thought I was after Kirk."

"Geez, she's the one who brought it up." Sarah flipped past another page. "So were you?"

"No!" (Sometimes I wonder about Sarah's selective listening tendencies.) "Of course I wasn't after him; they're engaged for heaven's sake. So I took Leslie aside one day and said I had told her a lie and wanted to apologize for it. I told her that in all honesty, I did not think Kirk was cute."

"Then what happened?" Sarah stopped chewing her gum.

"Well, of course you can't win on that," I said. "These are the kinds of questions that make horse races and wars. So Leslie got all bent out of shape and now she *really* won't speak to me. Haven't you noticed?"

Sarah thought for a minute. "She spends so much time with Kirk I hardly see her anymore."

"The minute I told her that I didn't think he was cute, I could see the whole future scenario. For the rest of their lives, they'll remember how one of Leslie's roommates didn't think Kirk was good-looking. They'll tell the story, embellished more each time, in every new ward they move into when they're asked to speak in sacrament meeting and include how they met. I saw all this in an instant, and it was still too late."

Sarah smiled. "So you don't think Russell is cute?"

"I never said that."

"You didn't say he was, either"

"And I'm no longer in this conversation," I said. "In two more minutes, this tape will self-destruct and I won't even know who Russell is. Or who Sarah is."

Sarah laughed and put up her magazine. "I really should be writing to Doug, anyway."

"Who's Doug?"

"My missionary. But don't tell Russell."

I put down my book and covered my ears with my hands. "Say no more," I said. "I'm outta here." With that, I went into the kitchen to get some cold pizza.

I was so tired of hearing about Kirk, Russell, Doug, Tom, Dick, and Harry. I sat at the kitchen table and chewed on my pizza. What was going on here? Had we all passed through some kind of force field that makes you lose all sense of individuality and convinces you that you have to be heavily involved in at least one romance to have personal worth? Were our hormones on a reckless rampage? Or were we competing in some kind of ludicrous contest? Why were all my roommates, and most girls I knew (myself included), so preoccupied with dating?

Could it be that some girls are insecure and are seeking approval? Does it validate them just to be invited out, even if they aren't particularly attracted to the guy who asked them? This is dangerous, because then—to make the approval worth something—they have to convince themselves that his opinion is particularly valuable, so they put the guy on an artificial pedestal. When they do this to themselves, their self-esteem sinks even lower; they need approval even more, and the cycle just spirals down and down.

I like what Hugh Nibley said: "The only person you try to impress is your Heavenly Father, and it is awfully hard because he can't be fooled—not for a minute. I have always felt driven in this way. The gospel is so wonderful. There is so much to find out. It opens the doors to so many things. It is sort of an obsession, a sort of personal thing. As long as you are going to be doing something, why not be doing something that hasn't been done before?"

Yet so few of us can truly say that Heavenly Father is the only person we're trying to impress. I guess when we can honestly say that, we'll know we have sufficient self-esteem. (By the way, if you know anyone whose self-esteem could use a boost, recommend service.)

I'd overheard dozens of conversations in my two years at BYU, and far too many centered around guys. Granted, many girls were also immersed in exciting schoolwork and other activities, but more than a healthy percentage seemed to define their worth based upon whether they had a date for Friday night. It was almost a "date or die" mentality.

I decided right then to go cold pizza. I mean cold turkey. I wasn't going to stop dating, but I was going to stop *worrying* about it. In fact, the notion of taking a break from circulation sounded wonderful. Who wants to be circulated, anyway? It sounds like something that should happen to a corpuscle.

It was the best I had felt in months. For once I was going to take seriously the advice that we hear all through the Church's Young Women program: develop your inner strengths and talents so that when marriage does happen, you'll be prepared (and so that if it doesn't happen, you'll still be happy).

I got out my Young Women card, a little worn now, but still dear to me. I read the seven values, and remembered how I'd embroidered a bouquet of flowers on a pillow just a couple of years ago, each blossom in one of the colors assigned to the values. Every night as I'd turn back my bed, I'd place the pillow on my bureau. And I'd look at the flowers and remember the values. It meant so much to me. It still does.

What had I done recently to grow in Faith, Divine Nature, Individual Worth, Knowledge, Choice and Accountability, Good Works, and Integrity? I got out some paper and set some new goals. It felt like coming home again. How could I have let these slide?

(Ironically, the girls who do work on developing and nourishing their spirits—instead of securing a weekend date—are the ones who invariably get asked out most often.)

Never again was I going to accept a date just to be "going out." In fact, for the first time it hit me that wasting a guy's money and time like that can be downright cruel. Not only do you keep him from dating someone he can have a real relationship with, but you lead him on and use him. Not fair and not nice.

Besides, when you date someone you're not excited to get to know, you'll probably be a boring date. You think people can't tell when your heart isn't in it? Ha!

"Filler dating" also keeps *you* from better pursuits, like self-improvement, studies, service, and other things.

Emily dated a guy named Jake last year. About three months into their hot romance, Emily's engines cooled. She really wanted to break up with him, but kept putting it off. "After his birthday," she'd say, or "Not now—not with Christmas just around the corner." There was always some holiday or activity that provided an excuse to keep dragging out the relationship. There was also some security in knowing she had a steady date all the time. Jake became her "filler boyfriend."

Finally, one night when we were talking, Emily explained that she had always been such a kind, sweet person that she didn't have the strength to hurt anybody.

"Emily," I said, "I need to say something to you that might sting a little bit."

Emily glanced up. "What is it?"

I took a deep breath and prayed that I'd have the spirit of love when I spoke. "What you're doing isn't kind or sweet. Emily, you are hurting Jake far more by lying to him than you would be if you broke things *off.*"

Emily was shocked. "I've never lied to Jake!"

"Letting him think you love him is a lie, Emily. Lies don't always have to be spoken; just the intent to deceive is a lie," I insisted.

"But if he doesn't know, how can that hurt him?"

I was surprised at my roommate. "Because it's just a matter of time before he does find out. What are you planning to do—marry him and live this pretense for the rest of your life?"

Emily frowned. "No. I guess I was hoping Jake would lose interest first."

"Emily," I said, as gently as I could, "That's selfish. You want him to be the bad guy and give your guilt a holiday. Think about what you're doing. You're letting Jake fall more in love with you every day and you're taking up his life. If you let it go much further, he'll have a hard time ever trusting anybody again."

Quietly, Emily began to cry. "I guess if I really cared about Jake, I wouldn't have let it go on so long," she admitted.

I hugged her. "It's easy to put it off when you know something will hurt somebody. But in choosing not to break up, well, that's a choice, too. And in the long run, it hurts a lot more."

Like so many of us, Emily had gotten into a dating rut and needed to push the pause button. Most of all, she needed to reevaluate her motives for dating. Was she looking for a husband, a good time, or just a way to fill her Friday nights?

Some girls date because they have a kind of panic about marriage. Again, that old thorn—low self-esteem—makes them worry that no one will ever want them or find them attractive. They're so thrilled when someone finally expresses some interest in them that they leap into the fellow's arms and hang on for dear life.

Let me explain why this is wrong. First, this antsy nervousness about being "an old maid" presumes that singleness is always awful and marriage is always great. None of us should be so naive as to think marriage will solve all our problems and make us happy. I heard a Know Your Religion lecture once, and the speaker said that people who have discovered how to be happy as singles are the same ones who end up happy as marrieds. And if you can't find fulfillment and joy in the gospel and in your own unique wonderfulness by yourself, a spouse isn't going to do it for you, either. It's the kind of thing, like a testimony, that you have to earn individually.

This same speaker said that if you had to list the four states of adulthood in order of desirability, they would be (1) Happily Married, (2) Happily Single, (3) Unhappily Single, and (4) Unhappily Married. It quickly becomes obvious that the key is to enjoy the state you're in, whether married or single.

I know a number of single women here on campus who are older and have never married. And, though they look forward to the day when they can fall in love and marry, they aren't moaning and moping about it; they're getting on with their individual growth and having a marvelous time of it. They travel, they pursue interesting hobbies, they have loads of friends. And they have great faith that the Lord is watching over them.

One of them gave a talk about fitting into a "family church," and said she was almost afraid to admit what a great time she was having. For her, church activity was based entirely upon one thing: Is the Joseph Smith story true? And if so, then the Book of Mormon is true and the Church is true, and whether a ward dinner gives family discounts is completely beside the point.

"Who cares if on Mother's Day the Primary girls forget to give me a carnation?" she said. "I grab one of those little kids by the arm and say, 'Hey—I'm a future mother; I'll take one of those,' because I know I'll either be a mother in this life or the next. And, through Eve, every woman alive shares in that general motherhood." (I liked this gal's spirit.)

Then she said, "I feel so blessed just to have an answer to my prayer about whether Joseph Smith was a prophet, that all the trappings and social activities simply do not matter. Oh, I go to them, and I have fun as a matter of fact. But I'm active in the Church because I have a testimony of the restored gospel."

Then she quoted Joseph Fielding Smith: "My advice to our girls, if you cannot find a husband who would be true to his religion and have faith in the gospel of our Lord, it is better to abide in 'singleblessedness.' It is better to suffer some denial in mortal life and receive life everlasting than to lose your salvation in the kingdom of God. Remember the Lord will make up to you in joy and eternal union more than you have temporarily lost if you will be true and faithful."

I was so glad that a lot of young women heard that talk; I think it took the desperate edge out of dating.

Of course, we all hope to have perfect lives, happy marriages, good children. And people who postpone marriage in order to live selfish, hedonistic lifestyles, or because they refuse to grow up and accept responsibility, are cheating themselves of the most refining school of growth your spirit can ever attend. Marriage is a commandment, and not one to be taken lightly.

But again, because it is so very important, no man or woman should feel that they must rush into it without thought or inspiration. This goes back to the girls who panic and get married just because they're afraid no one else will ever ask them. It's kind of like interviewing for a job. Some people have so little confidence that they go into the interview just hoping and praying to get the job, instead of approaching the interview as the two-way street that it really is (i.e. "Do I really want this job?" "What kind of company is this?") Yes, you are being checked out, but you should also be checking out the company.

And so it is with marriage. You don't just say yes because someone has finally asked you; you evaluate them and pray about whether it's a wise move. When you have this attitude, you don't date in a panic anymore, just to keep from sitting home. Sometimes it might not hurt to ask yourself, "Would I have more fun at home alone?" And often the answer might well be yes!

You know what I did? I went for several weeks without a single date. Whenever a guy would ask me out, I really thought it over. Did I see any potential at all here? Would my time be better spent another way? I wasn't being overly critical; I was just finally being realistic.

And when at last I did date again, I did so in definite moderation. Plus I dated only guys I could honestly say I liked and admired. There was sense in it. (Direction is so much more important than speed.)

Meanwhile, I think I made myself into a more desirable companion (I certainly got more offers, I know). I plunged into academics, sports, and scripture study. I thoroughly enjoyed my talents and hobbies. I took time off just to play. I became a better friend, giving time to girls instead of just guys. I prayed with more conviction, and listened better now that I wasn't in such a hurry. I pondered and meditated.

I even had one date, Brian, tell me he felt honored to date me. I laughed. "Be serious," I said.

"I mean it," he insisted. "Everybody knows you won't date just anyone—you're choosy."

I smiled. "That's right. I select my dates choosily. I choose my dates selectly? Hmm . . ."

Brian put his arms around me. "Louisa, you're the only girl I've met who seems both anchored and spontaneous."

"Yeah, well, contradictions are my life."

"Hey. You asked me to be serious, and I am. Don't you see how unusual you are?" (I decided not to comment on that question.) Brian went on. "You're fun and bubbly, but most girls like that are . . . I don't know . . . flighty and skittish. Not you. You also seem smart. No, it isn't smart. What's the word I'm looking for?"

"No, it's smart," I said, trying to slip in an extra compliment.

Brian laughed. "I mean, it's like wisdom or something. I know you take your schoolwork seriously, but it's like you take your religion even more seriously."

"Thank you, Brian," I said. "I do."

And suddenly I realized that going off to college is not just a move you make to find a husband. It isn't something you do because everybody else is doing it. Going to school is something you do because it's vital to your personal growth; here is where you not only learn your major, but things of *major importance.* And while marriage is important, the dance steps of dating are not. Finding the right spouse is one thing, but being the right spouse is essential. And just "going out" doesn't do much to advance you on that path.

It reminds me of Proverbs 4:7, where it says, "Wisdom is the principal thing; therefore get wisdom: and with all thy getting get understanding." If we learn everything in our textbooks, yet fail to live better lives for it, we're nothing more than programmed computers. And if we date up a storm, yet fail to improve ourselves along the way, we're nothing more than wind-up escorts. We should evaluate ourselves and our dates, not just the movie we're going to see.

I'm not saying that the minute a girl turns sixteen and starts dating, she should get out the old clipboard and start analyzing who would make a good husband. At first, dating just teaches us basic social skills through fun recreation. It's merely friends having a good time.

But eventually, dating takes on different meaning and you begin to think about that old expression that you marry someone you've been dating. You look at your dates differently, and you *do* think about potential mates. That's when you begin to wonder what kind of parent your date would be, how dedicated to Christ's teachings they are, and whether there's friendship and physical chemistry between you.

Dating stays fun (sometimes even more fun), but it becomes a more serious business—the business of really picking the right companion.

CHAPTER ELEVEN

Looking for Orville Skidbottom

Wouldn't life be simple if dating were computerized? I don't mean those dating services where you fill out a form listing hobbies and interests, and they match you up with somebody insufferably like yourself. (The wizard who conjured up that method obviously never dated someone who was truly like himself; you almost always end up either bored or competing.) Also, what's the fun of dating a mirror image? It's our little differences that bring zest and variety to our lives.

The least promising concept I ever heard of, was a dating service that a guy developed for pet owners. "That way," he reasoned on a radio talk show, "you'll date someone who likes animals the way you do." Right, I thought. You'll fall for a guy with two Dobermans, both of which would like nothing better than to eat your poodle for breakfast. It's tough enough being compatible with another person, but can you imagine trying to get your cats and dogs to get along? Anyway, the kind of dating computer I'd like to see is one that employs wisdom and common sense—an unfortunate deficiency in electronic equipment. You'd tell it your life's story, then lights would flash, bells would ring and presto! It would spit out a little piece of paper with your beloved's name on it, and a convenient phone number.

But, alas, the most important decision we will ever make in our lives comes with no such software. We're on our own. However, we're not left entirely in the dark. In fact, we're not even in the shadows very much. There are so many excellent resources and formulas to make it easier and to shed light on this big step. First of all, there's prayer. Nothing in this world tops personal revelation, those promptings from the Holy Ghost that are available to all who seek them.

And there are the scriptures. Now that might sound a little far-removed from your having to choose between Rufus and Rupert, but really it's not. The scriptures, especially the Book of Mormon, are *filled* with advice on this. Well, maybe not Rufus and Rupert specifically, but you know what I mean. In the New Testament, Paul says tons about marriage. In the Doctrine and Covenants, there's so much good counsel that if all you did was read what the Lord said to Emma Smith, you'd have a beautiful formula for marital success. And there are other books and experts offering good advice, too. Though I'm not in a hurry to marry, it never hurts to learn what you can about the process before you're standing on the brink of The Big Decision without so much as a map.

Let me share with you some little goodies and ideas I've picked up in my travels through Datingdom. First of all, consider Lowell L. Bennion's incredibly easy formula, the ABC method. It works for guys or girls. Let's assume you've found someone you'd like to date regularly. We'll call him "A." Now, instead of just seeing "A" exclusively, you begin to date "B" also. You don't try to hide it, but you see them both over the same period of time. You can also add "C" in there. Now, should your relationship with "A" or "B" stop, you can add on "D" or "E."

But you never date more than three different people during the same period of time. When you get ready to think of marriage, then you can get serious with someone you've known for months, along with other guys, before you make your choice.

I wish I'd known about this method when I dated Joel (obviously Joel was using the A to Z method). But the ABC method has many advantages. For one thing, it allows you to compare people simultaneously. You hear a lot of squawking about how unfair it is to compare people, but I say baloney. Of course you have to compare people when you're dating; how else will you ever make a decision who to marry? If you only date one person exclusively, you risk being interested in him just because he's a guy, instead of for his specific traits.

This method also keeps you from getting obligated sooner than you may want to. You reduce the risk of someone assuming too much, and you can back away more gracefully than from a steady boyfriend.

Another benefit is that it keeps you from dating just one person steadily, and prevents you from dating "a multitude," as Brother Bennion puts it. Best of all, it encourages friendships before affectionate involvement. Especially when you're young, dating should really just be about friendship, not heavy romance.

Back in my Joel days, Barbara sent me a list that I found very helpful and which I'm sure I'll refer to again. It's a list of six ways to learn everything you need to know about a man before you marry him (and leaves me wondering what a comparable list about women might be). Anyway, consider these: (1) Watch him drive in heavy traffic, (2) Play tennis with him, (3) Listen to him talk to his mother when he doesn't know you're listening, (4) See how he treats those who serve him (waiters, maids), (5) Notice what he's willing to spend his money on, (6) Look at his friends. Then if you still can't make up your mind, look at his shoes. A man who keeps his shoes in good repair, generally tends to the rest of his life, too. I don't know. There's nothing on that list about how to tell whether Mr. Wonderful is falling in love and contemplating marriage to somebody else (Joel would've aced that list), so it isn't completely foolproof. Also, it doesn't mention sex, religion, in-laws or parenting—four big topics to discuss before you slip those rings on. But still, I think the list is interesting food for thought.

President David O. McKay, whose incredible romance with Sister McKay is legendary, had a standard that sounds pretty solid. Here's what he said: "In choosing a companion, it is necessary to study the disposition, the inheritance, and training of the one with whom you are contemplating making life's journey. You see how necessary it is to look for the characteristics of honesty, of loyalty, of chastity, and of reverence. But after having found them, how can a young person know when he or she is in love?"

President McKay continued, "A fellow student and I considered that query one night as we walked together. As boys of that age frequently do, we were talking about girls. Neither he nor I knew whether or not we were in love. Of course I had not then met my present sweetheart. In answer to my question, 'How may we know when we are in love?' he replied, 'My mother once said that if you meet a girl in whose presence you feel a desire to achieve, who inspires you to do your best, and to make the most of yourself, such a young woman is worthy of your love and is awakening love in your heart,' I submit that as a true guide."

David O. McKay also, in urging young people to marry in the temple (don't ever get talked out of that or do anything to cost you this essential blessing), said that when you do kneel across the temple altar to be sealed to your love for eternity, you have six assurances.

First, you know your marriage began in purity and cleanliness and that your children are guaranteed a royal birth. Second, you know your religious views are the same. Third, you know your vows are being made with the idea of an eternal union, not to be broken by petty misunderstandings or difficulties. Fourth, you know that a covenant made in God's presence and sealed by the Holy Priesthood is more binding than any other bond. Fifth, that a marriage begun this way is as eternal as love, the divinest attribute of the human soul, and sixth, that the family unit will remain unbroken throughout eternity.

What more could you ever want?

I like talking to people who seem to have made all the right decisions and earned all the best blessings. Our prophets and leaders would be in this group; there's so much to be learned from their advice. I try to read all that they've written or said, because I know they've not only *lived* their advice, but that much of their advice comes through revelation.

However, I also listen carefully to those who have stumbled and fallen; often they know exactly where they went wrong and they offer grave warnings that I hope to heed. Last summer I attended Relief Society with my mom in my old home ward and the lesson was on children who stray.

First of all, Sister Jenkins said that despite your best efforts, kids still have their free agency, and sometimes they let go of the iron rod and fall to the side. (A quick glance at the scriptures points out Lehi, Alma, Adam, and many others who had some rebellious children.) But then she said that just as there are times when it is no fault of the parent, there are times when a parent's mistakes do contribute to a child's transgressions.

One mother had previously volunteered to tell about her wayward family. After years of denial, she said she was finally able to admit that she'd made a number of mistakes. Boy, did everybody perk up and listen! First, she hadn't married in the temple, and her family life was filled with strife over church attendance. Next, she had missed valuable opportunities to teach her children when they were young, because she'd been busy pursuing her career. She had been far too lenient, she said, allowing them to talk back to her, not demanding from them the respect she deserved as a mother. "If I'd only had more self-esteem," she said, "I wouldn't have allowed any of those things to happen." (There's that self-esteem again!)

As we listened, her pain was right there, permeating the room. I thought about how easy it would be to follow in this woman's footsteps—she fell in love and made compromises, tried to give in and please her husband and her kids. But in thinking such flexibility was a virtue, she took it too far and allowed everyone to trample her. It was truly sad, but I was thankful to her for sharing her mistakes so that others could learn.

And it's the same with choosing a husband in the first place: sometimes by listening to those who have endured harrowing divorces, you can see pitfalls to avoid, and recognize danger signals before you make the same mistakes.

I talked to a divorced woman at BYU once, who said that when she was dating she had a list a mile long of all the qualities she wanted in a husband. "I didn't need a man," she joked. "I needed an encyclopedia!" She was looking for all kinds of details, she said, that clouded the more important issues. "Now that I'm a single mother, the top quality I look for in a man is whether he'd be a good father. And having been married to a man who wasn't, I now know exactly how to recognize one who is."

So often when we're dating, we forget to look for that trait. Yet it can bring so much joy or heartache, depending on whether it's there or not. Marion D. Hanks urges young people to choose their children's parents. "Though we could not choose or direct in our earliest days the home we grew up in or the parents who bore us," he said, "we can do something about the sort of parents we are or will be, and about the home our children will grow up in."

Heather's dad gave her just one piece of advice about how to choose a good man. He said, "God gave us two ends: one to sit on and one to think with. Our success depends on which one we use most." He urged her to pick a man who's not only a hard worker in his profession, but who has energy for the marriage and for parenting. (In other words, "You snooze, you lose.")

Kelly asked her dad once for the best piece of marriage advice he could give. He was reading the paper at the time, and didn't even lower it to give his short, immediate answer. "Don't nag," he said, and turned the page.

It's good to think carefully (and more important, *prayerfully)* about whom you marry, but there are some people whose ideals and expectations are so terribly high that they can never accept another person—who, like all of us, comes with imperfections and weaknesses—and they never marry because they're too critical (a blessing for those of us who don't want to be buffed and prodded all our lives, but definitely a loss for the overly critical person).

My bishop gave a talk once called "Looking for Orville Skidbottom" about this very problem. He described a girl who was determined to have it all. She wanted a fellow who was a spiritual giant destined to be a General Authority, a traffic-stopper in the looks department, a Mr. Megabucks, an athlete who could get down on the floor and play with kids until he was ninety, a genius with an I.Q. of 240, a witty wonder who got invited to every party ever thrown, and a romantic lover who would bring her roses every day—the whole shebang.

For years she dated men who fell short of her lofty goals. Yet, she was convinced that every trait was vital and wouldn't settle for less. Finally after years of searching, it appeared her wait was over. For there, across the room in an English class, sat Orville Skidbottom, her ideal man. Handsome, rich, seemingly quite spiritual, athletic, smart, clever, and romantic.

After class she hurried up behind him and introduced herself. He was cordial, but didn't seem to realize that they were destined to marry. For weeks she threw herself at this fellow, all to no avail. "You see," said the bishop, "it seems Orville Skidbottom was waiting for Gertrude Frumpbucket."

It reminds me of the time I arranged a date for two friends I knew in high school, Kathy Shuman and Jeff Finkley. Both of them sneered at me later for setting them up with someone so unattractive.

And just as some people err in being too fussy, others aren't fussy enough. They decide to marry the first person who stirs within them any passion, convinced that this is not just revved up hormones, but a direct revelation. They forget that if you fall in love with someone's eyes and aren't careful, you'll wind up married to the whole person.

Even if you do your best to listen to both heart and head when you're dating, and you do in fact marry someone you feel is the ideal companion for you, I guess we should expect that there will still be surprises and rough spots to work through.

That's why, when we're looking for our mate, it's so important to include in that list of "essential traits," the quality of being able and willing to talk through problems. I've heard so many people complain about issues in their marriages that they should be able to discuss and work through with a willing spouse. But too often people pout, storm off, pull up silent walls, retreat into shells, and simply refuse to *talk*. And yet time and again, I've heard happily married (and happily remarried) couples say that this willingness to talk is "everything." I know I sure look for that in my dates.

My brother Bill and his wife, Wendy, had this kind of problem. Scarcely a year after their wedding, they ran into a snag. Suddenly the beaming couple who posed on the temple steps for a photo that could have convinced even the most anti-marriage rebel to get his life in order and get married like that, found that married life doesn't just coast from the temple to heaven's gates. Sometimes you have to get out of the wagon and push.

I had called Bill, who was working as a pharmacist now, to ask him about some new drugs. Now, now, lest you jump to the same conclusions my trusting roommates did, these were not drugs for *moi*; I just needed some information for a report I was writing in a health class.

Anyway, as he answered my questions, I detected a tone of sadness or something in his voice. "Bill, is anything wrong?" I asked.

Then he told me that he was afraid Wendy just didn't care about him as he had thought she had. "I've been working at this new pharmacy for five weeks now," he said. "And do you know she hasn't once asked to come and see where I work?"

He felt heartsick that his wife had no more interest in him than that. Here he was, working all day to support them, and she hadn't so much as asked to peek in and see the place. To Bill, this was the ultimate rejection—proof positive that he had married an unfeeling, unsupportive woman.

"Well, have you asked her to come and see it?" I asked.

"Louisa," Bill said, as if I had rocks for brains, "She knows I go to work everyday. She *knows* where I am. I shouldn't have to send her an engraved invitation."

Whenever someone talks about engraved invitations, watch out. I don't know why, but it usually signals trouble. Somebody is hurt, offended, or refusing to give in.

"Would you like me to call her?" I figured it couldn't hurt for a little sister with a great track record of muddling things up to poke her nose into it and make matters worse.

"No way," Bill said. "I'm not going to give her the satisfaction of knowing how much this has hurt me."

"What satisfaction?" I said. "How could it bring a wife satisfaction to know her husband is hurting? Do you really think Wendy is looking for ways to belittle you and make you feel bad? Bill, pull yourself together here and talk to her."

"Nope," Bill said. "You can talk to her if you want, but I'm not going to bring it up." (I don't know where he got that stubbornness; it couldn't be from *my* family—ha ha.)

I agreed to call Wendy, under Bill's condition that I just test the water, not come right out and tell her the problem. Since Wendy and I get along great and talk frequently anyway, I figured this would be fairly innocent and easy.

Wendy answered on the first ring. "Oh, I thought you were Dr. Cheseman," she said.

"Who?"

From her voice it was obvious that Wendy had been crying. "It's a marriage counselor, but don't tell Bill."

I was stunned. "A marriage counselor?"

"Oh, Louisa," Wendy said and burst into tears. "I just don't know where to turn. Bill's been working at his new job for five weeks now, and not once has he invited me to come and see his new pharmacy. He's probably ashamed of me and doesn't want his coworkers to see me. I've never felt so hurt, Louisa."

(Have you ever wanted to laugh so bad that your teeth hurt, but you knew if you did someone would kill you?)

"Wendy," I said, trying to sound as serious as possible, "have you told Bill you'd like to see where he works?"

"Of course not. I'm not going to *beg,*" she said. "If he wanted to share that part of his life with me, he would. I shouldn't have to push my way into places where I'm not wanted."

"But maybe Bill doesn't know that you'd like to see where he works," I suggested.

"Oh, of course he knows. He's my husband for heaven's sake," Wendy said.

"And so he should be able to divine all this through ESP, just because he's your husband?" I asked.

"Well, no," Wendy stammered. "But it won't be the same if I have to ask; it's like inviting yourself to a party."

"Wendy, you and Bill need to talk more. You're both assuming so much and you're both wrong."

"What do you mean both?" Wendy asked. "What's he assuming?"

I sighed and decided that if I can forgive Bill for humiliating me in front of Mr. Cooper, he could forgive me for breaking my word and telling Wendy everything. So I did.

"Don't you see?" I said. "You've both jumped to crazy conclusions when all you needed to do was share your honest worries."

Wendy was almost giggling she was so happy. She wanted me to tell it all over again, especially the part about how much Bill wanted her to see the pharmacy.

"No, you call Bill and get *him* to tell you," I said. "Not only is this long-distance for me, but I think anybody who's all jazzed about seeing a pharmacy probably needs more drugs than they have in one."

But Wendy wasn't listening. She was all twirled up in the phone cord, probably planning a romantic dinner for two that night (while I, the Fairy Godmother who had waved my magic wand for them, was relegated to leftover chili.)

But I gave a lot of thought to Wendy and Bill's situation, and realized I've done the same thing with my boyfriends. It's so easy for misunderstandings to creep in; that's why talking is so vital.

Like most couples, here were two people from completely different backgrounds (despite having nearly everything in common that is possible). Bill's expectation is that the wife makes obvious, outward inquiries into his work. Coming to see his workplace means she cares. And to Wendy, doing that is pushy. To her, a loving husband would just automatically pull his wife into his working life. It's just how they assumed marriage would be, or the way they were raised.

And then, of course, they both made rash assumptions without checking with their spouses, always a big mistake. It's so important to ask if what you're worried about is true. Even if you think your partner will see it as a silly, little thing, you should bring it up. Despite its seeming silliness, it's important to you. And if you don't get it out and get rid of it, it will grow and compound. Anytime there's silence—trust me—the worst will be assumed. You really owe it to the other person not to hold in your dark suspicions. All relationships function better when they're kept healthy and aboveboard. (Plus, when we assume the worst, we're almost always wrong. How nice to get reassurance from a loving mate that we had nothing to worry about.)

That night Bill called me, that dreamy little-kid sound in his voice, as if Wendy were tickling his ear as he spoke (and she may well have been, for all I know).

"Hey, Louisa," he said, "I wanted to thank you for helping us patch things up. I guess you think we're pretty funny, huh?"

I smiled. "Yeah, pretty much."

"Louisa!"

"No," I said. "But sometimes I think you two are a little too much alike for your own good."

I heard some whispering and giggling, then Bill said, "What? I'm sorry. Wendy was talking to me." I laughed. He hadn't heard a word I'd said, and it was just as well.

"Keep her talking," I said. "That's the best news I've heard all day."

CHAPTER TWELVE

The Undate

Now I ask you: How many times should a girl have to swing at a golf ball and miss, before she has paid sufficient dues into the dating machine, and can retire?

Where's Jeannie when I need some athletic tutoring? I'll tell you where she is; she's back East going to college, attending a great LDS institute, wearing the make-up and hairstyle *I* taught her to do, dating the neatest guys in the world (so she says in her letters), and leaving me stranded in the top of the Rocky Mountains with dates who insist upon sporty activities.

You want irony? I'll tell you irony. Irony is Jeannie, the woman in whose little toe exists more athletic prowess than most guys will ever see in a lifetime—being taken to operas and concerts which she hates, and I would love. Meanwhile, I—who would adore an evening at the ballet or the symphony—find myself dressed in the very sort of clothes I despise (namely, sweat suits), bounding clumsily about on a racquetball court and getting smacked in the leg with the ball every fourth hit or so.

I have so many purple bruises on my body, I look like I've been in a plum fight. Should I ever fall down the escalator at the mall and knock myself unconscious, the paramedics will take one look at my multicolored body and say, "Look! Someone attacked this poor girl and beat her to a pulp!"

It isn't that I dislike all sports—just the ones involving high-speed balls . . . or low-speed balls. I truly don't understand why otherwise intelligent people want to walk about in an area where projectiles are being launched. Seems to me there ought to be barbed-wire fences and military warning posters around or something. HIGH-SPEED HANDBALLS—GO BACK! Or NOW ENTERING GOLF BALL ZONE—PROCEED AT OWN RISK.

I do like skating and horseback riding. I just never encounter any *guys* who like those things.

We should all meet at the luggage terminals at the airport. That way I could avoid the kinds of guys who travel with golf bags or racket-shaped carry-ons. (And Jeannie could meet her dates there, too, and go for the guys who carry duffel bags of athletic wear as opposed to tuxedos in garment bags.)

I've even tried to excel at ball sports. Okay, sometimes I don't try as hard as I used to in high school. Back then, I had no idea that I was completely devoid of hand-to-eye coordination. I went into every new sport expecting to do well (confidence is the feeling you have before you fully understand the situation), and feeling utterly surprised when I didn't.

But today, old and wise twenty-year-old that I am, I have a more accepting outlook. The reality of my "unathleticness" has settled onto me and seeped under my skin like a tattoo that reads "KLUTZ" in big, bold letters—refusing to budge and looking for all the world like a permanent condition.

So I have come to accept this minor deficiency in my dowry, and to like myself immensely despite it. In no way does my self-esteem suffer over this (you probably noticed), and I also figure I have other qualities to offer my ideal man, who I imagine is mature enough not to care that I can't hit a ball. In fact, he may even find this characteristic cute or endearing.

"Impossible," Darin says, but I've heard more incredible tales than that.

I suppose, if you had to rank all the kinds of dates there are in order of effectiveness (that is, if they teach you what this person is *really* like), sports would rank pretty high. Just as going to a loud dance or a movie leaves little opportunity to get to know a person, I must concede that sports are quite the opposite, and teach you a good deal about your partner.

In my case, I get to see immediately whether the guy is patient, or whether my klutziness infuriates him. I can see at once whether he expects us to be the same or allows room for differences. I know right away whether he's a fierce competitor or an easygoing pal.

(In Jeannie's case, since she nearly always beats the guy at whatever game he suggests, she gets to see how good a sport he is and what his attitude is toward women who win all the time.)

And, conversely, if a guy plays sports with me, he discovers that if he wants an athletic companion, he'd better take this one home early. Also, he gets a golden opportunity to learn whether he enjoys teaching, or if he resents waiting for others to catch up.

Sports teach you how a person reacts both in winning and losing (sometimes a gloating winner is even harder to tolerate than a sore loser). They teach you about tempers, humor, cooperation, and attitude.

I watched Jeff Trenton play church basketball once. I noticed there was another guy on the team, named Sandy, who played the way I do. (I never said this was a championship team.) Every time Sandy missed, I noticed some of the guys going through motions of exasperation; I even saw some of them look at this fellow when he was wide open, and then deliberately throw the ball to a heavily guarded guy who they simply thought was a better athlete.

But not Jeff. When Sandy threw and missed, Jeff was right there to pat him on the back. Jeff gave him encouragement in little ways all through the game, almost like a father or a coach. He passed the ball to him often, and when the guy missed one particularly easy shot, Jeff immediately shouted, "It's okay, Sandy. Next time!"

I wasn't in love with Jeff, but I recall thinking that his future wife and kids would be lucky to have a guy like that, someone who really cared about other people's feelings, someone for whom team spirit meant more than just winning.

So, much as I'd rather see a movie than slug some volleyball into the air, I have to admit that sports teach both my date and me more than the mere rudiments of the game.

If you're just dating to do something fun, then I don't suppose it matters how "educational" your dates are; you're not in the market for a mate yet, and you aren't trying to learn the true character of another person. But for those taking the more serious courses (Advanced Placement Dating or Vocational Dating), you're ready to find your one true love and settle down.

This is when you need dates, likes sports and games, that really teach you something about yourself and your partner. I call these the Undates, and I've decided that in addition to the big info return on your investment, they can be even more fun than the superficial dates.

And speaking of games, those are good Undates, too. Have you ever sat down with a group of people to play some board game or even a parlor game, and one person is dead serious and out for blood? Heather dated a guy like this once. He *had* to win. And heaven help you if you beat him once or twice. The rest of the evening you had to endure his sniping little comments that betrayed his thinly veiled and growing hostility. Playing games with people definitely reveals their personalities.

Probably the best Undate of all is working on a committee with someone. Ask any divorced person you know, or anyone unhappily married, if they wish they'd been able to work alongside their spouse for a few months before marriage, and I'll bet they give you an immediate "yes." It seems that so much of marriage involves working together, that this—more than any other single activity—tells you if the two of you are compatible.

Also, it's hard to conceal personality weaknesses in the workaday world; you really see someone in all their moods and phases. Now I realize that it isn't always possible to work full-time at some job with your sweetheart, but you can certainly work on limited projects or committees together.

Do a church service project (clean up an elderly widow's yard, mend her fences, paint her house, etc.) or volunteer to work on a political campaign. Design a big school fund-raiser together, organize other people, build a shed for a farmer, wallpaper a bathroom, even make a video (sometimes the more creative a project is, the more our artistic egos get involved).

Work together on something that requires a lot of compromise and sacrifice. See how you feel about dividing duties, and which tasks you're willing (and unwilling) to do.

There are always charities, schools, hospitals, and organizations who need volunteers. Pitch in and see how the two of you blend when there's work to be done. Is one of you lazy, compulsive, indecisive, bossy, or unreliable? Better find out now. But you won't only encounter negative tendencies; you'll see positive ones, too—both in your partner and in yourself.

Sometimes activities like this awaken noble traits within people, virtues that they didn't even know they had: the knack of being able to laugh when all goes wrong, compassion with those who are discouraged, leadership that motivates others to pull through, discipline, stamina not only for physical work but for mental work, generosity, real love of fellowman, patience, problem-solving skills, and much more.

And remember how I told you that service is the key to self-esteem? Well, at the very least, you'll come away from a project like this feeling super about yourself.

Eugene England, a former BYU professor, talks about how both marriage and the formal organization of the Church are "schools of love." In his book *Why the Church Is as True as the Gospel,* he explains how both institutions force us to grow, learn, make mistakes, grapple with tough relationships, be hurt and then forgive, be stretched and challenged, and ultimately be made better. He says that the very things that sometimes make Church so trying (dealing with difficult people) are the things that make it so vital for our salvation—because without those obstacles, we'd never learn tolerance and sacrifice and all the other essential traits we need for exaltation.

And, to a great degree, committee work teaches you some of the same things. It's almost scary to think of marrying someone you *haven't* worked alongside.

Another good Undate is a study group. I was in one for an economics class I took, and the assortment of our personalities was classic. First, there was the brainy guy who felt burdened by having to meet with those less intellectually gifted. He did a lot of weary sighing.

Next to him sat a girl who was highly organized and very impatient with anyone (namely me) who cracked jokes or tried to lighten up the serious atmosphere she was determined to create. She wanted everyone there on time, pencils sharpened, notebooks open, mouths shut, and assignments read—or off with your head.

Then there was me, admittedly in way over my head in a subject I thought was much simpler than it is. ("What can there be to economics?" I'd said as I registered for this torture. "You open a store, you sell a product, and you deduct the cost of your product from the money you take in.")

So rather than sob and cry and admit I have no brain for business and beg the others to work privately with me so I could catch up, I decided to dance witty little steps around them, making horrible puns, ridiculous wisecracks, and trying to look smarter than I actually was.

Another guy in the group was a natural leader and automatically fell into the role of teacher, calling on various members to talk, and basically being the "camp director" of our gatherings.

One guy was extremely nervous, wanting to repeat and review until you could scream. "I just want to make sure I have this straight," he kept saying, as if he were a spy getting the exact directions for an ambush that would save freedom as we know it.

Another guy wanted to begin and end each study group with prayer, cross reference each topic to his scriptures, and rely upon the Spirit to guide him at test time.

One girl was determined to shine as the best and brightest, and defensively kept interrupting with statements such as, "As I was saying—if anyone would ever listen to me—" "See? I was right again—that's the fourth time tonight—" and "I already said that ten minutes ago. Why didn't anybody agree with me *then?*"

Needless to say, no marriages resulted from that mismatched little study group. But we sure got well acquainted.

Some Undates I particularly like are church activities. Not only are you "standing in holy places" and participating in activities that bring you closer to God, but you are finding out whether your partner shares the same level of commitment that you do. Going to church with someone, while it doesn't allow for discussion at the time, gives you plenty to talk about afterward. And church activities such as parties and other social functions let you see how your partner reacts in a group.

Occasionally a church activity is of such a sacred or spiritual nature that we need to be careful. We have to be careful not to misinterpret the tremendous and strong spiritual feelings that result from the Spirit there as a witness that our companion is The One. He or she may well be, but we need to recognize intensely spiritual feelings as the separate events that they are.

Another good Undate is simply a new environment. Sometimes it helps to see your companion in a different setting, away from your usual turf. In high school I dated a guy who was voted "Most Charming" at the end of the year. He'd been involved in team sports, service clubs, and fraternity-type organizations. Around other high school guys he was an obvious leader and relished his power. But when I invited him to a party at my dad's office, he stood in a corner with his hands in his pockets. Suddenly he wasn't the star of the show, and worse than that, he admitted that he didn't have the first idea what to say to "grown-ups." It was almost as if he shrank before my eyes.

The way someone acts on campus or in their old neighborhood might be completely different from the way he'll act once you marry and he gets a job transfer to Michigan. People often act differently away from their families, too. Some families have strong roles that each member is expected to play, and a fellow who was always giving in to his domineering family might find new strength when he can get out from under those smothering dynamics.

Haven't you ever noticed how, no matter how old a person gets, they still behave like their parents' child when the folks come around? I look at my mom, who's definitely strong and capable at home (always seeming to make the right decisions), and what happens when *her* mom shows up. Suddenly my grandmother is telling my mother what to do, as if Mom is a child, and my mother is actually letting her! They're still playing the same roles they always have.

So a person who feels overwhelmed on a huge campus might become a tower of confidence in a small town. Someone who enjoys the social whirl of immense school popularity might become subdued and even depressed when all that attention is gone. Or, you might find that you've chosen a partner whose personality is pretty steady and unchangeable. You just never know until you try it.

Another good Undate is the excursion. Share something you enjoy with someone, where both of you can talk. Go on a country hike, a bike ride, or visit a museum. Stroll along and share unhurried laughter, dreams and goals. I walked along the beach with a fellow once, and found him so fascinating that before I'd even realized it, we'd gone three miles down the coast. We picked up shells and bits of rock that he later made into a beautiful mosaic for me, so I would always remember the day. Little did he know I would remember it anyway, simply because we'd had such a wonderful talk.

And I guess that brings us to talking itself, with no distractions. Sometimes simple *conversation* can be an Undate. My Uncle Verl's entire courtship with his wife consisted of his coming over to her house and visiting with her. (He jokes that her parents didn't want her alone with him for even one minute, and if you knew how wacky my Uncle Verl is, you'd know why.) But in those living-room chats, they fell in love. In time, Uncle Verl was like a member of the family; they didn't just sit on the sofa—he pitched in and helped cook and do dishes, repaired plumbing, helped younger kids with homework, and cheered up anyone who was sick. In short, his sweetheart got to see him in real action, doing the very kinds of things he'd do as a husband. Uncle Verl had no money for special dates, but he'd think of novel ways to surprise her nonetheless. One time he arranged the living room to look like a puppet theater and he put on a show for her, complete with popcorn.

I'd love to have been a fly on the wall that evening. Family folklore has it that Uncle Verl got halfway into the melodrama when he realized he was short one puppet. So . . . he popped up into the "window" and pretended to be a puppet himself, pantomiming the movements of a marionette. (Uncle Verl never took a drama class in his life and is no small guy. He must have been hilarious).

Just think of all the moods and personality traits my aunt got to see in Uncle Verl (and married him anyway, I tease him.) Theirs was truly a friendship before they married, just as it should be.

I like the Undate of sharing an interest or hobby together. Maybe you both like oil painting, dancing, playing musical instruments, or working puzzles. It may be that you both enjoy test-driving racy cars, collecting coins, growing plants, or making crafts. I've met couples who liked animal-training, mystery-solving, and photography. Some people share a mutual love of archaeology, playing the stock market, mountain climbing, or genealogy. And I suppose your common interest could even be (cough, cough) a sport. You know where your interests lie; sometimes our lives are enriched when we can share these special loves with *our* special loves. Just be aware that every one is an individual and needs separate pursuits, too. Let's face it; if you both want to read the same novel at the same time, you're asking for trouble. As long as your private hobbies don't form a distancing wedge between you, they can actually make you more interesting to each other.

Joel and I had a situation like that. I'm now able to look back on that relationship and appreciate some of the good times. I can also see some lessons it taught me, and one was allowing each other room for individual talents. He liked writing music at the piano, and I liked needlepoint. Both were private activities and we'd have been pretty unrealistic to insist upon sharing these together. (I don't know a half-note from a half-back, and Joel's interest in handwork stopped just short of tying knots in his shoelaces.)

But, despite having no native talent in those areas, we could both appreciate the other's skills. Joel was amazed at the intricate pillow I stitched for his birthday, and nothing could have pleased me more at the time than the love song he wrote for my birthday.

My parents, as I mentioned, love trying new restaurants. Eating out is more than a way to fill your stomach for them; it's a hobby. At the end of every meal, they sample three or four desserts, then rate them. I've even seen them hold the winner high as we all cheered, slapping the person on the back who had the good sense to order it. Mom and Dad always confer before they order, agreeing upon two dishes they'd both like to have (and halve), then they share with each other. (Never have you seen two people who enjoy their food more than my parents.)

But maybe I've inherited a little of that, because I really enjoy cooking with my dates. Now I realize that there are legions of men who could lose the kitchen in a meteor storm and not notice it for two years. (My dad, for example—though he loves to eat out, he hates to cook.) But there are also guys who truly enjoy tossing a pizza crust into the air, throwing together their special barbecue sauce, or whipping up a flaming glaze for a sundae. These guys definitely know the way to my heart.

Nothing seems more romantic to me than making something delicious with the one I love. I picture us laughing together, getting flour on our noses, snitching creamy raw cookie dough, and inhaling the heady fragrance of fresh-baked bread. To me, the kitchen is the most romantic room in the house.

But I also realize that, just as I have an aversion to some sports, there are countless guys out there who feel completely out of their element when trapped in a kitchen. Suddenly they are no longer in charge, and they even feel a little stupid. ("Maybe now," I said to one of them, "you know how I felt trying to throw that football last Saturday.")

However, cooking is far easier than learning to play most sports, and if non-cooks start with something fun and simple, they can experience a sense of grand achievement in a relatively short period of time (say, five minutes for a chocolate malt).

Also, life can go on without sports (even though there are those who would argue), but it cannot go on without food. And I'm pleased to report that I have converted many a cookaphobic into a guy who can't wait to impress friends (usually other dates, since I've already seen it) with his raspberry cheesecake, veal scaloppini, lobster bisque, and apple dumplings.

Hey. It's the least I can do for my fellowman.

CHAPTER THIRTEEN
Glop Principle

Toward the end of my sophomore year, I fell in like again. Joel had faded into a ghost of boyfriends past, and I had even caught a glimpse of him (okay, okay, it was while I was shopping in the mall) after our breakup without feeling one emotion in any direction— except for a little sympathy for his bride: what kind of husband would Joel be for her, if he couldn't even be honest during their courtship? But now romance was in the air again—quite literally— as I began to see a fellow who, among other things, was a pilot. Cliff would take me flying over gorgeous canyons and lakes that seemed so secluded, I felt certain we were the first humans (in spite of the occasional tents that I chose to ignore) ever to glimpse such breathtaking sights.

And Cliff was a breathtaker himself. He wasn't handsome in the traditional sense, but he had such class and style that it made you swoon just to be around him. He was from some wealthy Connecticut family and simply oozed sophistication. (I even learned the right way to pronounce a couple of words, just from listening to Cliff.)

He'd been on a mission to Africa, spoke exotic languages (in addition to what he called "Prep School French"), and was getting his MBA. He ordered endive salad and asked if the chef could stir a teaspoon of tarragon mustard into the dressing. His shirts had his monogram on the cuffs, and he always sent them out to be cleaned and pressed, rather than ironing them himself.

He used embossed stationery with gold foil linings in the envelopes and sealed the envelopes with personalized stickers. (When I blurted, "Wow—neat stickers!" Cliff chuckled and said, "They're not stickers . . . they're *seals.*")

He wore a Rolex watch and actually carried calling cards which he kept in a silver case from Tiffany's. The house he rented in Provo, with two friends just like him, had a living room filled with Chippendale furniture, a cherrywood display case filled with polo trophies, and a refrigerator filled with seven imported cheeses.

Looking into Cliff's refrigerator, I felt like Barbra Streisand in *Funny Girl*, when she discovered that Omar Sharif used seven different toothbrushes, one for each day of the week.

When I told Cliff I was thinking about joining an exercise club when I go back to California for the summer, he assumed I was joking and laughed. "Can you imagine if you really did that?" he asked. "That's like publicly admitting you don't have your own gym." (Now I thought he was joking, so I laughed.) It was only a week later that I discovered he not only had his own home gym, but stables, tennis courts, the works. And he naturally assumed that "everyone from California" has not only those same amenities, but a private surfing beach as well. (Lest you think him incredibly naive, let me tell you that he got this impression from the various hoity toity Malibu friends who'd swing through Connecticut on their way to the South of France to visit Cliff's prominent father.)

"How on earth did you survive a mission to Africa?" I once asked him. Cliff shrugged and mentioned that he'd been to Africa on safari several times, and that Kenya was in fact a favorite vacation spot of his father's. (I should have known.) I imagined Cliff on his mission, seeing the whole experience as a jolly good outing and even wearing a pith helmet as he taught investigators. Elder Adventure.

I must admit that I allowed Cliff's jet-setter style to impress me. I felt somehow more literate, more well-traveled, and more well-bred when I was with Cliff. Class by association, perhaps.

I was using the ABC method of dating at the time, but A and B were no match for C, and soon I was dating Cliff exclusively. I had even reasoned that I could be falling in love and why should I lead A and B on, wasting their time and mine?

One week Cliff, who knew I was a pushover for a guy who cooks, offered to whip up a gourmet dinner for me. He had a driver pick me up and deliver me to his house, which was filled with pink roses everywhere you looked. His roommates had both gone out for the evening and Cliff had turned their house into the inside of a French candy box.

The table looked ready to be photographed for *Architectural Digest*. China, crystal, silver—even napkin rings. (Wow—guys never think of napkin rings, I thought to myself.) In my life I had never seen such a lavishly decorated table. Cliff, in a stunning white dinner jacket (I sound like I'm moderating a fashion show, I realize, but the man did look dazzling), pulled out my chair for me. Then he disappeared into the kitchen for appetizers.

I looked at the centerpiece—some of the roses had been dipped in gold. Beside my plate was a tiny box containing a chocolate truffle, and next to that was a bottle of expensive perfume, tied with a red satin ribbon. (No, I did not squeal, "Whee—party favors!") Above my plate I noticed some pink embroidery on the tablecloth. Looking closer, I saw that in gorgeous script it read, "Louisa." Holy cow—he even had the tablecloth customized for this dinner!

My mouth was still hanging open as Cliff brought in course after course of delicious food. Suddenly it hit me: Cliff has designed this beautiful setting and this phenomenal food because he's going to propose to me, and he wants the night to be special. What will I say? We've only known each other for seven weeks—I need more time! He hasn't even met my parents. I haven't met his. Am I in love or just swept off my feet? Is Cliff the right one? Help!

After dinner, Cliff led me to the sofa, where I figured he had probably stashed a ring the size of Kentucky. He held me and we began to kiss. "You seem nervous," he said.

"I am," I admitted, still mentally groping for a way to tell him that I need more time before I can commit to marrying someone.

He began to kiss my neck and whispered, "This is your first time, isn't it?"

Well, the nerve of him, I thought, assuming that this is my first proposal! I thought of saying, "I've been proposed to *lots* of times." (Not entirely true, but why let him think he's chosen somebody no one else wants?) Finally I just said, "Maybe."

Cliff looked into my eyes and smiled. "I can tell it is. Don't worry, darling. I'll teach you everything."

Suddenly a cold chill ran down my back, and I could feel myself turning to stone in Cliff's arms. My heart nearly stopped. "Cliff," I stammered, not believing what he had just said, "What are you talking about?"

"Come on," Cliff said, pulling me from the sofa and down the hall, "I want to give you one more gift."

By now we had reached his bedroom door. I pulled away, nervous. "Cliff, this evening has been so perfect. You don't need to give me any more gifts. Really."

Glancing into his room, I could see candles flickering, and the silvery sheets had already been turned down. The soft music I'd been hearing all evening had been coming from a stereo in there.

I closed my eyes, and mentally—spiritually—somehow—reached out to my Heavenly Father. Help me, I cried out into what seemed like galaxies of dark space. Don't let me do this, I prayed. Please, Father, get me out of here. This is wrong, all wrong.

I had always told myself that should I ever find myself in a situation like this, I would recall 1 Corinthians 10:13, and that scripture came to my mind like a reflex: "There hath no temptation taken you but such as is common to man: but God is faithful, who will not suffer you to be tempted above that ye are able; but will with the temptation also make a way to escape, that ye may be able to bear it." Where was my escape hatch?

Cliff was pulling me close in the hallway now, his lips against my ear. "It's just you and me," he said.

Tears welling up in my eyes, I prayed for the strength to resist him. All evening, with every perfect morsel of food and every fragrant bouquet, Cliff had been wearing down my defenses. Suddenly I needed my Father in Heaven to lean on, to take my hand, to give me courage.

He didn't let me down. In my desperate reaching for the Spirit, it was right where I'd left it before. I was suddenly filled with an overflowing gratitude that I knew, really knew, my Savior and how to reach Him. We'd been through so much together, and I had worked so hard on that relationship. I loved Him unspeakably and couldn't let Him down.

I pushed Cliff away. Hard. "No," I said, sudden strength in my voice. "No, it is not just you and me." I was crying now, and my words cracked through a swollen throat. Cliff looked astonished.

"You can't hide from the Lord," I said. "I feel Him with me often, and he knows everything we do."

Cliff threw his arms around me. "Oh, Louisa," he said, beginning to cry. "Please don't say no to me. I couldn't stand it. I'm so crazy about you. I've never met anyone like you in all my life—"

For just an instant, I wanted to comfort him. Cliff suddenly seemed so lost, so lonely. Some nursing instinct inside me wanted to say, "Oh, all right. Just don't cry." But I drew the Lord close to my heart and had the strength to push Cliff away again. This time it was even easier. "What are you talking about? You're the one who said you'd teach me. Sounds like you've met lots of Louisa Barkers before!"

"It isn't true," Cliff said. "I won't say I've never done this before, but never with someone I loved. I really love you, Louisa. With all my heart."

Part of me wanted to gaze up into Cliff's eyes and purr, "Really?" But again I reached out in silent prayer. Please, Father, give me the words to say. I could feel even more strength as I allowed myself to be filled more and more with the Spirit. (Granted, sometimes we only allow a drop of the Spirit at a time into our often unwilling souls. But this time was different: I was inviting it in by the cupful.) "Cliff, you'd say anything right now to get me to go to bed with you. If you really loved me, you'd feel so protective of me that you'd never allow such a thing to happen." My heart ached, I was so disappointed in him.

Now Cliff decided to wear me down with sheer passion and began climbing all over me and kissing me. "But I'm helpless when I'm around you, Louisa. You're irresistible. You turn me into a locomotive, I swear—"

"Well, this is going to be a train stop," I said, suddenly stronger than I've felt in a long time. I pushed him against the opposite wall. "Cliff, you need to repent."

Cliff's tears suddenly dried up and he smirked. "Oh, come on," he said. "You think I'm going to tell my bishop—who's some Podunk farmer—about my background?"

And now my tears really came. They were streaming down my face. But instead of feeling weak and afraid, I was burning with righteous anger. "How dare you make such a condescending remark?" I said, raising my voice. "What's wrong with farmers? President Benson was a farmer!" Suddenly I felt the urge to dash out, grab the nearest farmer, and marry him just to spite Mr. Big Bucks. "You're nothing more than an overblown, selfish snob."

Cliff's nostrils flared. "Is this how you thank someone for an evening like that?" He pointed angrily down the hall toward the dining room.

"Oh, I get it," I said. "You set me up! This was nothing more than a calculated move to get me into your bed. I can't believe it! You're a returned missionary, Cliff. How can you act so—so—worldly?"

"I thought you liked the worldly things about me. You certainly had no problem riding in my Ferrari—"

"Wait a minute. Okay, I'll admit to some materialism. I was wrong to be so impressed by your stupid little car. That wasn't one of my spiritual high points. But that doesn't mean you can *buy* me."

A sneaky grin spread across Cliff's face. "Ah. You like to play hard to get. Hmm . . . I presumed a lavish dinner would do the trick, but if that's not sufficient . . ." Now he smiled, eager and filled with ideas. "I'm not a man to turn down a challenge. This weekend. We'll fly to Miami. From there to the Bahamas should only take—"

"Stop it!" I shouted. "I'm insulted. How dare you take my standards so lightly, never mind your own. I sure misjudged you, Cliff. And you *really* misjudged me. I'm sorry if I gave you any indication at all that I would agree to this sleazy little plan of yours. I'm leaving."

I grabbed my purse and headed for the front door.

"You're making a big mistake, Louisa," Cliff called after me.

"Is that a threat? If so, fine. Bring in the Money Mafia or whoever else you've bought and paid for. But I am not making a mistake. I am avoiding one. A big one."

Cliff grabbed my arm as I was heading out. "I must say," he said in his high-society tones, "I question a woman who'd turn down all that I can offer."

"Well, you won't question me for long, 'cuz I'm outta here." I felt brimming over with power, strength, and more self-esteem than had ever surged through my body before. "And the only thing you can offer is snob appeal. I'm looking for a lot more than a fat wallet, Cliff. I'm looking for a man who loves the Lord—and me. You don't love the Lord or you wouldn't take His commandments so lightly. And you don't love me or you'd respect me more. You love only yourself."

Cliff smirked. "Quite a speech, Sister Barker."

I shook my head, started off down the walkway, then turned around. "I thought you were so exciting, Cliff. You seemed to have so much class. But you know what? You don't have any class at all."

I walked a few blocks, found a pay phone, and called Emily to come and pick me up. "I can't believe I actually thought he was going to propose to me," I said to her, after the adrenaline had worn off.

"Are you embarrassed that it took you so long to realize what he was saying?"

I thought about that. "No," I said, feeling good and strong again. "I'm *proud* that I didn't know."

Emily smiled. "Yeah," she said. "Yeah." She gave me a thumbs-up.

I've often thought about that evening with Cliff and the various tactics he used to try and wear me down, one after another. It was as if someone had given him a list of my very weakest points. He knew precisely which buttons to press, like a professional seducer or something.

First of all, I love fancy, gourmet dinners and if the guy cooks it himself, it all but knocks me out. I'm crazy for roses, and Cliff knew that pink ones were my favorite. He knew that I like a certain brand of perfume, he knew the kind of music I like—he even knew I appreciated embroidery!

And when none of these ploys worked their magic, he moved instantly to my next button: tears. I always crumble and give in when somebody cries, and Cliff knew it. Then he professed true love, something every woman wants. From there he moved on to pure passion, another of my weaknesses. Next, he tried flattery. Then he tried to make me feel guilty, as if I owed him something for the lavish dinner he'd made. When none of it worked, he just plowed straight ahead and tried to buy my affection with yet another extravaganza: a trip to the Bahamas. And when still spurned, he questioned my judgment in turning down all he could offer.

I felt as if I'd been in a debate with Satan, and in many ways, I suppose I had. It isn't hard to guess which way Lucifer wanted the evening to end.

I thought about my various other dates who had done some of these same things in hopes of wearing me down, and how easy it must have been for them to figure out my buttons. Without consciously meaning to, we all indicate our weaknesses and preferences just in our day-to-day conversations. When we show particular interest in a certain compliment, we let others know that this is a sensitive and special area for us. And if people truly care about you, they respect and even protect those vulnerabilities; they never try to exploit them or use them as weapons to get something they want.

We each, including guys, have different buttons. And people like Cliff press whichever ones they think will work. (It isn't just young men who get overly amorous, either—many girls are even more aggressive than the guys are.) For some, the strongest persuasion would be a dare. Others might give in to someone more insistent. Still others would cave in to the argument that "everyone else is doing it." And many compromise in order to get something else—a job promotion or some other favor.

One of the most transparent ploys—yet amazingly the one that so few people can see through—is the argument that "if you loved me, you'd prove it." The immediate response to this should always be, "And if you loved me, you wouldn't ask me to give up my virtue."

You've read the column "Dear Abby" right? Abby says, "Girls need to prove their love through illicit sexual relations like a moose needs a hat rack. Why not prove your love by sticking your head in the oven and turning on the gas, or by playing leapfrog in the traffic? It's about as safe.

"Does he love you? It doesn't sound like it. Someone who loves you wants whatever is best for you. But now figure it out. He wants you to commit an immoral act, surrender your virtue, throw away your self-respect, risk the loss of your precious reputation, and risk getting into trouble." Anytime intercourse takes place, despite birth control, conception may take place. Transmission of diseases may take place. There is no such thing as safe sex.

Abby goes on, "Does that sound as though he wants what is best for you? This is the laugh of the century. He wants what he thinks is best for him; he wants a thrill he can brag about at your expense. Love? Who's kidding whom? A guy who loves a girl would sooner cut off his right arm than hurt her. In my opinion, this self-serving so-and-so has proved that he doesn't love you. The predictable aftermath of proof of this kind always finds Don Juan tiring of his sport. That's when he drops you, picks up his line, and goes casting elsewhere for bigger and equally silly fish."

Of course, today I'm sure you could refer not only to Don Juan, but to Donna Juan, for there are just as many cases now where it's the guy who has to be the policeman, trying to resist the advances of his girlfriend.

One of the saddest situations is when a girl—or a guy—has already gone farther than they should have, and they think, "Oh, what's the use in stopping now? I'm already ruined." Sin has hammered their self-esteem down so low that they figure it's too late to recapture their chastity. Really, it's not too late. Repentance is a cleansing miracle, and when transgressions are serious, bishops can help those who've stumbled get their lives on track again. Don't ever feel it's too late for you or that you can never conquer the shame and remorse of sin.

Those who would lead us astray are very crafty; they know exactly what our buttons are, and they even use this very argument. You've already done such and such; why are you suddenly putting the brakes on? I heard Jeannie's Uncle Barry give a talk to divorced and widowed members when I was visiting them. And this was one of their biggest problems—their dates all assumed that since they were no longer virgins (having been married), they should no longer "save" them-selves. Some people don't realize that sex outside of marriage is *never* okay. People who are determined to get what they want from you (and it really is a very selfish position), know exactly where your weak spots are.

Even the strongest among us have weaknesses that Satan knows and tries to pounce upon at every opportunity. I was talking with Emily about it, and she confessed to having a super strong need for approval. For her, when a guy offered physical affection, it was the ultimate form of acceptance. Whether she had feelings for the guy or not, she had a hard time resisting the validation it represented. But while she hungered for his attention, she also had great resentment that she even *had* that need and wished she could overcome it. She didn't feel rebellious toward the Church or the commandments; she felt trapped by a craving she couldn't control. Knowing that she was on very thin ice, and doing far more than she ought to, made her feel even more depressed and more in need of approval.

As we talked, Emily began to cry. She begged me to help her resist the temptation she always felt inside. Did I know any way for her to be strong? Whenever a guy gave her one compliment—even a transparent one—Emily would melt. It's a tribute to the strong standards of many faithful LDS guys that Emily hadn't already committed some serious transgressions.

"How can I say no, Louisa?" she asked. "I've heard all the talks about how important it is to stay morally clean. And this might sound contradictory, but I believe them. At least, intellectually I do. I know it's a serious commandment and I even know all the clever ways to say no that you hear in some fireside talks. So why can't I do it?"

This was a tough one and took some thought. "Maybe it's like drugs," I said. "I mean, with all due respect to Nancy Reagan, there's more to it than just saying no. Kids who take drugs have seen all the films and heard all the dangers; they know they're frying their brains and risking their lives, and yet they won't stop."

"You're right. That's the same way I feel about chastity," Emily said.

"Well," I said, "I don't think information about diseases or pregnancy is what keeps kids from slipping up. I think it comes down to one thing and one thing only: your relationship with the Savior."

Emily frowned. "But I go to church and stuff."

I tried to spell it out. "Emily, I've never worked harder at anything in my life than I have at really getting to know the Lord. It's more than casually reading the scriptures and saying bedside prayers. It's walking with Him, meditating, reaching out, and having faith. You need to study the scriptures seriously. Then fast and pray in a really spiritual way . . . maybe many times, before you'll feel especially close to Him." Tears came to my eyes, as I recalled all the times I've heard the still, small voice. To disappoint Him would devastate me.

"Emily," I whispered, "He really is there. Really."

She smiled. "You know Him, huh?" It was as if she were asking me about a friend of mine whom she wished she knew, too.

"Oh, Emily," I said, and suddenly hugged her. "Emily, He knows you so well you can't believe it. That's going to shock the pants off so many people, when they die and realize what a close, intimate relationship they had with Him."

Emily laughed. "The way you put things."

I wiped my eyes. "Emily, He loves you so much; I know it. He's just dying for you to reach out to Him—just wait until you make that connection; it feels like coming home. You're never lonely, you're never in the dark—it's beyond description how close and comforting it feels. If you can pray hard enough and really study and try to be guided by Him—" I took a big breath. "Oh, Emily! I want so much for you to know the joy I know. You'll overcome this approval thing and your self-esteem will skyrocket."

Emily was laughing again. "You get me all excited, Louisa. I really want what you seem to have." We both cried and smiled at each other for a few minutes.

"It's self-esteem, Emily," I said. "You've got to build your self-esteem through service, so you'll realize that every time someone flatters you, it's just . . . glop."

"Glop?"

"Yes," I said. "Glop. Next time some guy is pressing your buttons and complimenting you, I want you to really think about his motives, and think: Glop."

Emily laughed. "I sure have heard a lot of glop, Louisa."

I hugged her. "Yeah, me too. But now you're going to recognize it for what it is."

The next day Emily left a sweet card on my pillow, thanking me for being the kind of person she could confide in, and for loving her enough to share the solution to her problem. It was the first time in her life, she said, that she felt some hope.

At the bottom of the card, she drew the word "GLOP" surrounded by a red circle with a slash through it. Next to that she wrote, "My new motto." I was so proud of her.

And I watched her over the next few weeks, before we each headed home for the summer. I've never seen anyone work so hard to "call home." She prayed and studied, determined to weave into her life a closeness to Christ and the strength that would help her be moral. She memorized the Twenty-Seventh Psalm and whispered it softly to herself whenever she felt weak. She talked with the bishop and asked for special welfare assignments (this *really* boosted Emily's self-esteem; she would come home absolutely glowing).

Soon I noticed a little quote taped to the bathroom mirror. It was George Albert Smith, quoting Dr. Karl G. Maeser and said: "Not only will you be held accountable for the things you do, but you will be held responsible for the very thoughts you think." (Sarah stumbled into the bathroom bleary-eyed one morning, took one look at that quote, and slumped to the ground, groaning.)

Our bishop gave Emily a fantastic pamphlet called *Why Stay Morally Clean,* by Boyd K. Packer. It was a talk he'd given in general conference and contained so much good advice—what a find. Here are just a few quotes from him:

"There was provided in our bodies, and this is sacred, a power of creation. A light, so to speak, that has the power to kindle other lights. This gift is to be used only within the sacred bonds of marriage. Through the exercise of this power of creation, a mortal body may be conceived, a spirit enter into it, and a new soul born into this life." He goes on to say that this power is good—and not just an accidental part of God's plan, but an essential part. "Without it the plan could not proceed," Elder Packer says. "The misuse of it may disrupt the plan."

Then he tells us that this power had to have two dimensions: One, it must be strong, and two, it must be more or less constant. "Is it any wonder . . . that in the Church, marriage is so sacred and so important?" he asks. "Can you understand why your marriage, which releases these powers of creation for your use, should be the most carefully planned, the most solemnly considered step in your life? Ought we to consider it unusual that the Lord directed that temples be constructed for the purpose of performing marriage ceremonies?"

Elder Packer warns about Satan's determination to get us to use this power prematurely, and thereby lose our opportunities for eternal progression. He says that when you become a parent, you finally see what it is to love someone more than yourself. "Through this loving one more than you love yourself," he says, "you become truly Christian. Then you know, as few others know, what the word 'father' means when it is spoken of in the scriptures. You may then feel something of the love and concern that He has for us. It should have great meaning that of all the titles of respect and honor and admiration that could be given Him, that God Himself, He who is the highest of all, chose to be addressed simply as Father."

One night Emily and I talked about some other ways to avoid moral transgressions. First of all, you have to avoid the gray areas, because they lead to the black ones. Physical affection always wants more, and it's better never to get onto that demanding hunger track in the first place. Also, deciding ahead of time and praying for the Lord's help can make a difference. If you wait until you're swept away with passion to try to decide, you're asking too much of a mind that has already imagined you down the road several miles. Memorizing a scripture or hymn is good; they bring incredible strength when you're afraid.

Another good plan is to literally invite the Holy Ghost to be with you on your date. This doesn't mean you won't have any fun (as I told you before, I think God has an incredible sense of humor). It just means you'll have wholesome fun and go home feeling proud of yourself, rather than ashamed.

Emily had another idea I liked. She tries to imagine her future children. She pictures their little faces and hands, their innocence and purity. She sees herself as their mother and thinks of a beautiful family sealed together forever in the temple. She imagines a husband who trusts her and whom she knows she can trust, too. Thinking about this family really helps remind us of our priorities.

I saw her walking through the cafeteria recently, and I noticed something different about her. Not many girls used to like her, because she had a flirty edge to her personality. She used to make eye contact with every guy she passed, and subconsciously—and consciously—this put off other women. (No one except Emily knew the pain and neediness behind her flirting.) But today, despite getting glances from several guys, Emily didn't even see them and just walked right by.

I waved to her and she came over to my table. She was full of excitement over an audition for some school play, and as she chattered eagerly about trying out, two different girls passed our table, and both of them said, "Hi, Emily!"

"New friends," Emily whispered to me, proud and embarrassed by her new popularity. "I finally figured this thing out."

So far I hadn't said a word (that's so unlike me that I had reason to be proud myself). Emily went on. "I used to think women just plain didn't like me," she said. "But now I can see that I was so focused on getting attention from the guys, that of *course* the girls were turned off. So now, I hardly pay attention to guys. You should see me, Louisa."

Little did she know that I had already seen exactly what she was talking about.

"I'm so happy without all that glop," Emily said. "If I happen to talk to a guy, fine. But I don't need it now. Oh, Louisa, I feel like the Nephites when they were finally free—remember when they escaped—"

"You've been studying the Book of Mormon," I grinned.

Emily smiled. "Yeah! I didn't realize how much it applied to my own life. Who would have thought?" Then she saw another friend—a female one—across the cafeteria. "Oh—there's Marcy. I've got to give her some notes she missed. See you later!" And she was gone. I watched her striding confidently to her friend, smiling and almost floating above the crowds.

An angel could not have looked more at peace.

CHAPTER FOURTEEN

Falling in Love Without Breaking Your Ankle

Having a sister who's thirteen years older than you are can be a mixed blessing. On the one hand, she's older and wiser and gives you advice. But on the other hand, she's older and wiser and gives you advice.

That's kind of how it is with Barb. Sometimes I feel lucky to have an older sister who's already been through the things I'm going through. She has helped me and assured me that I would indeed survive Teen Trauma. But because she's so far removed from those concerns and is now PTA President and Mortgage Mama or whatever you become when you hit thirty, she snickers with Mom about the more youthful problems that *I* think are monumental. The two of them wink at each other and comment on how "cute" I am, the way you or I would say a baby is cute (depending, of course, upon the baby).

Sometimes Barb will shrug off something that *I'm* just not ready to shrug off, yet. Let me panic, all right? I'm a kid; I'm *supposed* to panic. True, I'm twenty now, but only on paper. Bill and Darin, now well into their mid-twenties, are getting "old and wise" on me, too. It seems they're always popping by to add finishing touches to the job of rearing me that Mom and Dad are now completing. Everybody wants to tweak the final product, you know?

Mom says I'm lucky; I can benefit from all the mistakes my siblings made. But how does it benefit me to know that Bill once crashed a speedboat, when I have no desire whatever to attempt stunt-boating? Instead, I was dealt my own individual bag of tendencies and I've been making my own little independent mistakes just as if I were an only child. None of my siblings ever wanted to date someone like Cliff, for example. They would have pegged such a person as a spoiled egotist right off the bat. But not me. I had to learn the hard way. And conversely, when I watch someone trip up in some area—Word of Wisdom, perhaps—where I feel no temptation, it only puzzles me since I can't relate to it.

(Just quickly, as an aside, I want to tell you why I've never felt tempted to smoke, drink, or take drugs. The real reason is Mrs. Benchley, a ninth-grade teacher I once had. She made us all work *so hard,* turning in volumes of weekly assignments—in triplicate and I am not exaggerating—that some kids even broke down in tears when she'd assign homework. She was daring us to succeed. Some kids crumbled, but I was determined to beat the meanest teacher in the world at her own game. I lived like a mole, never seeing the sun. I only studied. Well, darned if I didn't pull out the only A in that class. Now. What does this have to do with drugs? It taught me that I was smart. I've always gotten good grades, but I've worked so hard on my poor little brain, that I'll be a gorilla's girlfriend before I'll let something into my body that's going to fool with my brain cells. You know what I mean? I may not be an Einstein, but hey—I've earned what brainpower I have the hard way. It's sort of like having braces on your teeth. After going through all that agony, no way are you going to blow it now and forget to brush. You follow?) Anyway, I was saying that I haven't been able to benefit much from the mistakes of my siblings because we seem to be so different. But basically my brothers and sister have all turned out well, a tribute to Mom and Dad, and also to their own efforts. I can say I feel pretty lucky to belong to this family, so when I can swallow my pride for long enough, I even listen to some of their advice. Sometimes. If it would be impolite to interrupt, let's say.

So when Barb and her family came to visit during the summer before my junior year of college, she brought—along with six suitcases—a bundle of advice "to share with Louisa, now that she's getting up there." Up there—twenty is up there?! Up *where?*

I overheard her saying this to Mom as I was helping Barb's four children into the house with their dolls, bears, books, backpacks, and other traveling essentials. Great, I thought. Barb is going to sit me down and teach me about tax-deferred savings, interest rates and insurance policies. (Last time she visited, she cornered me with a lecture on home economy, closet organization, and apartment know-how.) Barb's husband is an investment counselor or money adviser or something like that, so giving advice comes naturally in that family. He had to stay in Sacramento, presumably to dispense more advice, so Barb and the kids came alone.

But instead of just telling me what to do and how to do it, this time Barb had a package of stuff she'd been gathering over the years, all with me in mind. And it was *interesting* stuff. The kind of stuff I really like. I felt humbled that Barb would go to so much trouble for a little squirt like me.

Some of it was about planning a wedding, which gave us both a good laugh and which I decided to file away for future use. And some of the papers were recipes, which Barb knows I love. But most of the materials dealt with how to tell love from infatuation, and how to tell if it's really love at all.

Having had my share of fluttering heartbeats, this was the very kind of thing I needed for the next time I think I've met Mr. Wonderful.

We sat down one night after the kids were asleep—including Megan, who merely pretends to sleep, and then gets up to pour Tempera paint into all the toilets. Only tonight she appeared to be genuinely zonked.

We put a big bowl of buttered popcorn on the table, and spread out Barb's papers. Mom and Dad joined in, enjoying the chance to reminisce about their early days of falling in love. Between the booklets and expertise around the table, I think we made a comprehensive list of what love is and isn't.

It isn't feeling even more smitten when you're together; it's loving just as much when you're apart. It isn't being so obsessed that you can hardly eat; it is feeling so secure and happy that you eat sensibly. It isn't an inability to keep your mind on your work, or to concentrate or study. It is being able to study and excel more, because you want to work hard for your loved one; they bring out your best.

When you're really in love, it has taken time to grow. Love includes physical attraction that wants to please the other person and is partially based upon deep admiration and love for that person. You enjoy each other as friends as much as you enjoy the physical chemistry between you. But infatuation leaps quickly into bloom, sweeping you away in a current of lust and the basic desire for sexual gratification.

Love is respecting another person's individuality; infatuation is living your life through someone else, or expecting them to live through you. Love lets you be alone and not lonely; infatuation makes you want a solution for loneliness.

Infatuation includes feverish excitement and miserable uncertainty until you can be together again; love is confident and able to wait, filling you with warmth and security. Love is being able to show all sides of yourself to someone and know that they'll still love you; infatuation is afraid to show all and presents only the candy-coated parts.

Love is secure and independent, allowing each of you room to grow and differ; disagreements usually lead to compromise. Infatuation needs continual assurance of being loved and is very insecure and dependent. Disagreements often become quarrels.

When you love someone and others criticize that person, it sharpens your attachment. When you're merely infatuated, the opinions of others can make you doubt your choice. When you're in love, you are confident that you belong to each other. Infatuated couples experience feelings of jealousy.

When you're in love you have a kind, even disposition and a feeling of goodwill toward others. When you're infatuated, your feelings of desperation make you edgy and short-tempered. Infatuated couples sometimes find monetary greed in their relationships; couples in love are willing to struggle, share, and trust.

Some people are in love with the feeling of being loved. But real love is thinking of what you can do to show you love the other person, rather than counting the things they've done to prove that they love you. Some folks have a compulsive desire to feel needed. But while real love wants your companionship, it doesn't need it in the sense of being unable to function alone.

Some girls are simply determined not to be "an old maid." Yet until you can be happy all alone, you're limited in the amount of love you can give another person.

Some couples think they are in love, when all they are is in love with the prestige, position, or financial security they've found in a mate.

Real love would be just as strong without all the trappings. You're proud of your partner in any situation and that admiration shows.

Some well-meaning romantics give in and get entirely swallowed up and dominated. Others like feeling in control of another person, still thinking of themselves first. (These two types often find each other.) But true love is none of those things. It's not a unilateral arrangement where one person has all the power and the other is subordinate. It's caring as much about another person's feelings and wants as you do about your own—not completely forgetting yourself and becoming a non-person, but sharing and respecting equally. You're willing to give in to please him or her, but you also feel welcome to express a differing view.

And when you truly love someone, you don't want to control them; in fact, their strength pleases you.

When you're in love, there's room for differences on little things; these differences even delight you. But usually, you have the big issues in common. You share similar values and goals. You respect each other as children of God, and you each aspire for the other to become all that they can be (without pushing). There's emotional maturity. There's honest acceptance and an honest view of each other's strengths *and* weaknesses. You can grow together better than you could grow individually, each enhancing the other.

Do you recognize yourself or a partner in any of these descriptions? Boy, I certainly saw myself and some of my dates in them! I was a little chagrined to see that most of my feelings had fallen onto the "infatuation" side of the table, rather than the true love side. But a little embarrassment like that is good for you; when you realize your mistakes in judgment, it sharpens your abilities for next time.

I listened while Mom and Dad talked about the signs of truly being in love, then Barbara looked at me and said, "You know, Louisa, when you get married, you need to ask yourself two questions. The first one everybody knows and worries about: how do I know this is really love? But the second one is just as important and needs to be asked even if you *do* feel real love. Ask yourself if this is a good person for you. We can fall in love with a lot of people. Just knowing that you feel true love isn't always enough. What if you fell in love with a wife beater?"

"C'mon, Barb," I said. "Lighten up."

"No, this is really serious," she said. "A lot of my friends have divorced because even though they were in love, they picked a person who was destroying them somehow. The husband of one of my friends was abusing their children—it was terrible. And the very fact that she genuinely loved him made it even worse. It broke her heart."

Mom shook her head. "Barb is right," she agreed. "I've seen sad situations like that, too. You do need to be in love, but love alone is not enough. You have to be sure of a lot more than just that."

We talked about it for a few minutes, and Dad said, "One of the hallmarks of maturity is being able to realize that you don't have to marry someone just because you love them." And then, to liven up the somber tone that the evening had taken, he added, "I fell in love *lots* of times before I picked your mother."

Mom just rolled her eyes. "You didn't know a woman from a wombat when I met you," she told him.

Now Dad pretended to be truly puzzled. "You mean those aren't the same thing?" Barb and I both booed his joke, and Mom threw a handful of popcorn at him.

Then Barb—as if this were her last chance to impart marital advice before I sailed off into the sea of matrimony—said, "Oh! I almost forgot. You should also cover the 'Big Three.'"

"The big three?" I asked, knowing she was waiting for me to pull it out of her.

"Yes. I was reading an article about the three most common problems in marriage. I mean, you can't believe statistics. As a psychology major, you should know that by now—"

"True," I agreed.

"But anyway, this article surveyed marriage counselors and when I saw what they said, I thought, Boy, that is so true—"

"Let's cut to the chase, Barb," I said, wanting to end the suspense. "What are the 'Big Three'?"

"Sex, money, and in-laws." Barb had a triumphant look on her face, as if she had just reported the most important news tip of the year. Then, suddenly frantic, she turned to Mom and Dad. "I don't mean you guys, of course." Barb's face was a giveaway, though. "Honest. There's no problem with you two."

Mom and Dad winked at each other. "Oh, we know," Mom said. "Don't we, dear?"

"But of course." Dad gave Barb one of his "give-me-a-break" looks. Barb just shrugged sheepishly, and we all laughed and called it a night.

The next day Barbara decided to take the kids to the beach. An excellent plan, I thought. If you can get Megan to wear a swimsuit, then you don't have to frisk her for concealed weapons, jars of Tempera paint, or harmonicas that miraculously play ten times louder than any other harmonicas in the world.

When I walked into the kitchen, Megan was hammering a nail into the wall with a Barbie doll that she had undoubtedly brought along for this very purpose. She had Barbie by the ankles and was pounding the nail in with Barbie's head. Each hit made Barbie's golden locks jerk into the air, but I must say Barbie maintained perfect posture throughout the ordeal.

"You're going to give her a concussion," I said, as I got the orange juice out of the refrigerator.

"I know," Megan said.

I decided to leave our conversation right there. Obviously I had miscalculated. I had assumed that Barbie was the tool and hammering a nail into the wall was the objective. But no, evidently the nail was the tool and pulverizing Barbie's brain into doll dust was the objective.

Barb soon came rushing in, checking her watch and grabbing sunglasses and lotion off the counter. "Come on, you kids," she said, hurrying them out to the car.

"Barbara," I said, "no one is going to shut off the wave machine. This is Southern California."

She smirked. "I know, Louisa. But I want to get there before it gets crowded—Oh, Megan, what are you doing? Mom, do you mind if there's a nail in the wall here?"

Mom wandered in from the laundry room with a stack of beach towels for Barbara and smiled. "Oh, no, that's fine, dear."

Barb smiled, kissed Mom good-bye, and took off with the children.

"How can you say it's fine?" I said, turning to Mom. "You now have a giant nail sticking out of the wall at knee height."

"Oh, we'll just pound it in and paint over it," Mom said.

"I can't believe it!" I fumed. "If one of *us* had done that when we were little, we'd have pulled weeds for punishment until our hands bled."

Mom headed back into the laundry room and glanced over her shoulder at me. "It's remarkable how you never exaggerate, Louisa."

I looked back at the nail, which now looked the size of a railroad spike. "Well, I can promise you this," I said. "When *I* have kids, they will never act like that."

Now I could hear Mom chuckling in the laundry room again. "That's going to be another exaggeration, Louisa."

I cracked some eggs into a bowl and began whipping up my special teriyaki omelet. Dad, following his nose, soon came in and sat at the breakfast bar like a dog under the dining table waiting for a scrap.

I smiled at him. "Okay, I'll make them for everybody."

"Great!" Mom called from the laundry room.

"I sure enjoyed our talk last night," Dad said. "Hope you didn't feel too lectured."

The eggs sizzled as I poured them into the hot pan. "No, it was interesting," I said. "You always wonder how you'll know when you're really in love. I wish Heather and Kelly could've been here."

Mom came in and started making some toast. "Louisa, I have a feeling that when *you* fall in love, you'll know it. It'll hit you like a ton of bricks and you won't even remember what you're doing."

I laughed. "Hey—maybe I'm already in love. I forgot to put in the onions."

Mom handed me the bowl of chopped onions. "You know, we talked so much about falling in love, but nobody said anything about falling out."

"Huh?" I turned one omelet out onto a plate and began the next one.

"Well, last night I was thinking," Mom said. "I realized that I want to teach you something that can't be taught—how to recover from the crash if you *do* fall in love and it doesn't work out exactly as you had hoped."

"Gee, there's a pleasant thought," I said. "I'm not even in love, and you've already got some guy dumping me and breaking my heart."

Mom laughed and squeezed my shoulders. "It's just that so many people go through life flitting from one hot romance to another, always thinking that the next person will be The One. They never realize that falling in love has a reality side to it."

Dad cleared his throat. "Excuse me, but can that omelet that's just sitting there be eaten yet?"

I smiled and handed him the finished omelet. "What reality side, Mom?" I said.

"Well, after you fall in love there comes a time when you realize that it isn't perfect," Mom said.

"Hey, hey—" Dad said, his mouth full. "I resemble that remark."

Now Mom's eyes lit up. "But that's when the deeper joy really comes, if you can stick with it. That's when you find out that *creating* love is even better than the fluttery 'first love' of falling in love. Some people spend their whole lives trying to recapture that kind of dizzying sense of enchantment in a new relationship. They get bored and move on, never working at the kind of love that really lasts."

"I think I understand," I said, pouring the last omelet into the pan. "You're saying that falling in love is easy, but *staying* in love takes guts."

"I wish you wouldn't use the word 'guts,' Louisa."

I laughed, feeling that deliciously naughty feeling all children relish when they know they've thoroughly grossed out their mother. All my school friends' moms had language rules about not swearing, but my mom was much more picky than that. She was concerned that we all choose "dignified" words. This meant that you have courage instead of guts, saliva instead of spit, and perspiration instead of sweat. I gave her a hug. "But that *is* what you mean, right?"

Now Mom smiled. "Yes. That's exactly what I'm saying. And if you do fall in love—and then out again—I don't want you to be a quitter."

"Yeah," Dad agreed. "I know so many guys at the office like that. Instead of growing up and realizing that love really begins after the fall, they abandon their wives for someone who offers them that feeling of novelty again." He spread some peach jam onto his toast. "And then *that* one fades. They do this over and over, never realizing that when the infatuation fades, that's when they have their best opportunity to build lasting happiness with someone."

We said the blessing (Dad sheepishly apologizing for having already eaten half of his breakfast), then Mom said, "You know, Louisa, I've seen the looks on the faces of teenagers when you tell them that enduring love is even more thrilling than infatuation, and they don't buy it for a second."

I smiled. "Well, it is kind of hard to believe that anything tops that first week in a relationship when it's so new and exciting."

Mom's eyes teared up. "But that first level is nothing, Louisa. I mean it—and it isn't that I don't know that feeling. I remember it well. But the love you feel after you've really worked with someone—there's no way to describe it. You simply have to trust that it's there and then experience it yourself."

Dad, flattered and blushing by how much Mom loved him, was dabbing her eyes with his napkin. "Oh, you," he whispered.

"You're getting toast crumbs in my eye," Mom said, starting to laugh.

I smiled. Right there was the kind of love she was talking about. Free expression, comfort for each other, and even laughter when it backfired a bit.

I want a guy who'll get crumbs in my eye.

CHAPTER FIFTEEN

Quick-Draw to the Rescue

That summer I volunteered at a local children's hospital. I was thinking of working as a child psychologist ("How convenient," Darin said, "if someday you have kids who are anything like you"), and this seemed a perfect opportunity to give some community service and also work with children, maybe collect some research for a thesis.

Most of the kids would be there temporarily, but some of them were seriously ill and would never lead normal lives. I wanted to work with those kids especially, to study what makes some of them so beautifully, stubbornly cheerful, so filled with optimism and joy, while others in similar situations were not. I wanted to find the differences and then give to the sad ones some sense of inner peace and a love of life.

Our stake president was on the hospital's fund-raising committee, and he arranged for me to volunteer a couple of times a week. But after looking into the lovable, adorable faces of those sweet kids, I found myself dropping by twice that often, just to surprise some of them with a balloon or a new riddle. Soon I was in line at the toy store, buying crayons and puzzles for my new friends. I'd chat with young mothers at the library about which books are most popular with which ages. I even took in a bunch of my own make-up so some of the little girls could play dress-up. (This gesture left my mother standing in the doorway, dumbfounded, just staring as I drove off.)

This volunteer work quickly became the most gratifying thing I'd ever done. For years I had driven by this hospital, never imagining myself working there. On the few occasions when I thought about the young patients inside, I thought of it as a depressing place where families were torn apart by cancer and other terrible tragedies.

And now, I could hardly stay away from there. Yes, there were some sad, heart-wrenching moments when a few of the kids didn't make it. But there was also a strong sense of love in that hospital; people were pulling together, families were reaching out to each other, and the Spirit was stronger there than anywhere else I'd been. It was as if the children were little magnets, pulling me back to a fountain of love.

I learned so much from those kids! I saw them reach out, even in their own pain, to comfort one another. I saw them share their gifts and toys, pray for each other, and buoy up faith. One little boy named Griffin absolutely stole my heart. He had curly red hair and no front teeth. Griffin had severe heart problems, and I used to tell him it was because his heart was made of gold. Griffin would laugh, and since he couldn't say his S's, he'd say, "Oh, Louitha, you are tho funny. Nobody'th heart ith really gold." But his came awfully close.

And there was a darling little girl named China, who was just as frail and delicate as her name. She always wore a tiny pink nightgown with matching pink bunny slippers, and she carried a doll that wore an identical outfit. Every time I came to see her, she'd kiss both my cheeks and shake my hand. It was an odd little ritual that endeared her to me at once. China loved pretending, and she especially loved imagining she was a princess. Her chemotherapy had made her lose her hair, so I showed her how to make a cone-shaped princess hat with a scarf streaming from its tip. Between this and the sequined crown that we made (for when she was the queen rather than the princess), China was able to cover her little head and pretend royalty at the same time. She usually cast me as the witch or the prince in these fairy tales, always trying to convince me that my role, in fact, was the more desirable.

"You can be the wizard," she'd say. "And that's a good part, because . . . because wizards have lots of power." This was supposed to sell me on my menial role, and inevitably I would discover that while the witch or the wizard might indeed have some power, it would never turn out to be *quite* as much power as the princess had.

Twice a week the children were treated to a visit by Quick-Draw the Clown. He was a talented college student who dressed in a full clown costume and told hilarious stories to the children. He illustrated the stories on a big easel as he went along, and then he'd let the kids color his drawings.

Afterward, he'd go into their various rooms and draw wonderful likenesses of the children themselves, and always he depicted them looking healthy and full of joy. Quick-Draw, or Q as I nicknamed him, would ask them what they wanted to be doing in the picture, and then within just a few minutes, they'd have a drawing of themselves flying like Superman, scuba diving, riding a dinosaur, and doing all the other fanciful things children dream about. Quick-Draw was their hero and they counted the minutes until his next visit.

And so did I. There was something wonderful about this goofy clown who could make even the saddest child laugh. He seemed utterly at home with the children, enraptured with their stories and full of questions about their interests. He followed their health histories and made a special point of bringing by an extra little toy or surprise for a child who had just undergone a difficult procedure or treatment.

After his clown act was over, Quick-Draw took time with them, sitting beside their beds and stroking their hair, humming a lullaby to some of them, or just being there to talk with some of the others. Since many of the kids came from great distances, their families weren't able to be on hand, and Quick-Draw became like a wonderful big brother to them.

Nobody could read a story the way he could; his voice would change for each character, making even the starchiest nurses snicker as they passed by. And he'd always talk about the book afterward, asking the children what they thought about it and what they had learned.

Talking with adults he was just as entertaining. Q seemed to have a natural humor that would spring from the present situation. Have you ever known a funny person who had a set repertoire of comical lines and stories, but after you've heard them all they don't seem so funny anymore? Well, Q was just the opposite: the longer and better you knew him, the funnier he got. A few weeks after he started working there, Q's dog ran away. When he finally came home, Q told of his "prodigal dog," and how several young poodles had come to the door waving paternity papers. Q shook his head.

"Where did I go wrong?" he mumbled. "Can you imagine if dogs tried to trace their family trees? Well, first of all, they'd stop at the tree and probably never get around to the branches." Q always made ordinary events more interesting.

At night, after the kids were asleep and visiting hours were over, I often felt too charged up to go home just yet. It was as if I needed some transition time before leaving the gentle spirit of this place and heading out into traffic, billboards, and the outside world. Evidently Quick-Draw felt the same way, because we started having dinner together. His clown make-up and wig had become so familiar at the hospital, that no one even looked twice when they saw him in the cafeteria.

One night I noticed Q passing up some of the fresh fruit he usually took. "Past their season," he said.

I smiled at him, teasing. "And how do you know this, Farmer Q?"

"I was in 4-H as a kid," he said. "Well, actually, it wasn't really 4-H. It was really more like 2-H."

I laughed. "You lived on a farm?"

"No, I just entered our garden stuff in the fair. I wasn't very good at gardening. But I became popular with the local gophers."

"Did you say grocers?"

Now Q laughed. "No. Gophers. But it's funny you mentioned grocers. I worked in a grocery store in Hollywood for a while during high school."

"Really? What did you do?"

Q smiled. "I was box-boy to the stars." I laughed and he went on, "No, my real job was shopping-cart welder. They do have that, you know. Why do you think it's so hard to get the carts apart in the stores?"

I laughed again, and we sat down at a table. "So you're the culprit," I accused him.

"Guilty. Before that I worked as a Fuller Brush Adolescent."

"Oh, please."

"Not really. I just sold stuff door-to-door. Mostly gardening seeds. Had to keep up my image with the gophers, remember."

I shook my head. "You really worked a lot as a kid."

"Sure. Didn't you?"

I thought for a minute. "A little. Mostly I tried to get out of working." I buttered my roll.

Q looked at me with real tenderness. "I don't believe that," he said. "I've seen how hard you work here, and you're not even getting paid."

"What?!" I said, pretending to be stunned. "You mean they're not going to give us a big paycheck at the end of the summer?"

For a second Q didn't know if I was kidding. Then he squinted. "Almost had me that time," he said. "I've got to be quick to keep up with you." He took a sip of his soup.

"Well," I teased, "lucky you're Quick-Draw, then, huh?"

He grinned. "Yep."

"How do you draw so fast, anyway? You're so good at that. Well, you're good at everything, really. I've never seen a guy—a man—a clown—" I started laughing. "I'm sorry—whatever you are—anyway, I've never seen someone so good with kids."

He smiled. "Thank you. I like to think I've been given certain gifts. One of them is art; it's just an inborn talent and something I enjoy. And if I'm any good with kids, well I guess that's a gift, too. All I do is play with them." He shrugged, as if he truly had no idea how remarkable his talents were.

He asked me why I was volunteering at the hospital, and I gave him the long explanation of my child psychology research, my belief in volunteerism, and my plan to help the more discouraged children become happier and perhaps write a thesis on that.

"How about you, Q? Why are you here?"

He shrugged. "I just thought it sounded like it'd be fun."

I stared at him, then laughed. "That's why you're so good at it," I said. "Here I am struggling and analyzing and making such work out of it, and you're just having a good time."

Q grinned. "Louisa, that's something I always make sure of. No matter what I'm doing, I always have a good time."

I envied his philosophy. It didn't smack of wild abandon or hedonism, either. He just seemed determined to enjoy life. I got the feeling that if he were on a camping trip, he'd be the one cracking jokes and making sure everyone else's spirits stayed high. What a great outlook.

"Wanna taste some curtain soup?" he asked, pushing his bowl toward me.

"No thanks," I said. "Why do you call it that?"

"Because," Q said, "you eat it and *it's curtains.*"

I laughed, then leaned in to whisper. "Just like *all* the food here."

Q bounced his dinner roll on the table top, then caught it. "Hmm, I don't know *why* you'd say that, Louisa."

I started giggling and finally gave up on eating altogether. "I've gotta get home," I said. "See you Tuesday." Q winked at me as I left.

The next day, I had planned to play some games with a young boy named Jeremy. He had been following a difficult therapy plan to help him walk again. Every day he had to walk the halls, and each time he would wince in pain. But this day was particularly discouraging, and Jeremy refused to follow his therapy plan. He gave up and began bitterly sassing all the doctors and nurses. By the time Tuesday rolled around, Jeremy's spirits had sunk lower than ever. Since Q and I had become friends, often talking about the children, I was the first person Q would seek out in order to get news about the kids. This Tuesday I waited anxiously to tell him about Jeremy's discouragement. I figured Q would go in and get him laughing and in a few minutes everything would be fine again.

But today Q didn't smile. He whispered briefly with Jeremy's doctor, then went into Jeremy's room. I stood in the hallway, listening.

"Get out of that bed right now!" Q said. I was stunned. I'd never heard him speak so firmly. His voice was still kind, but you knew he meant business. "Come on, pal. We're taking a walk."

"No," Jeremy said. "I'm not doing it and you can't make me."

"We'll see about that." The next thing I knew, Q had picked Jeremy up out of bed and was carrying him into the hallway. Jeremy was kicking and screaming.

Q winked at me, as proud as a new father. "See that kick?" he whispered, as if he couldn't even feel Jeremy's feet pummeling his stomach. Two nurses stayed on either side, as Q forced Jeremy to walk the halls. While the rest of us had been trying to coax Jeremy into cooperating, only Q knew him well enough to know that in Jeremy's case, you had to get tough.

"I'm not doing it!" he kept yelling. But Q and the nurses just led him persistently through his therapy, and gradually Jeremy settled down, resigned to the reality of having to do his walking.

Now that the young boy had stopped shouting, Q was able to encourage him. "That's it, Jeremy," he said. "Look at that! Did you see that last step? That was phenomenal, buddy. You're doing it. All right!"

By the time they had circled back to Jeremy's room, he fell into Q's arms, crying and hanging onto Q's neck. "I love you, Quick-Draw," Jeremy whispered. I saw Q's eyes glisten.

He was encouraging to me, too. Once, when Griffin was having an operation, I sat on his empty bed and cried. I was so scared for him, so terrified at the thought that he might not survive. I touched Griffin's little crayon box, his cereal box magic ring. Surely his little hands would hold these things again, wouldn't they? I knelt beside Griffin's bed, weeping and crying. Soon I felt a strong hand upon my shoulder, and Quick-Draw was kneeling beside me. When I stood, Q held me. "He'll be all right," he said.

I had thought about sharing the gospel with Q. He seemed so spiritual already, so full of faith and so humble. I had even heard him telling one little girl about the way Jesus loved children so much. Imagine my joy at discovering that my new friend was already LDS!

Here we had spent hours volunteering at the hospital, we had talked about our common interests (he liked reading, too), we had shared our goals, we'd discussed the work at hand, yet neither of us had ever mentioned our religion. I had only found out that Q was Mormon when a bishop came by to give a blessing to a little boy with kidney failure and asked if Quick-Draw could assist him. (It was understood at the hospital that Quick-Draw was never to use his real name, so the children could believe in him as a real clown, a real magical character). It was one of the most beautiful blessings I'd ever heard, and it gave great peace to the boy's family, too.

Later, though he seemed reluctant to give any details, Q did tell me that he had served a mission and was now studying to become an architect. I'd never seen Q out of costume, but as crazy as it sounds, I began to think of him as handsome. One day as I was driving home, I laughed aloud when I realized I was daydreaming about a clown with a big red nose, red circles on his shiny white cheeks, black stars on his eyes, a giant red mouth, and an orange wig. Yet by now, we all loved Q and somehow saw beyond his costume to the beautiful person beneath it all.

I thought about the various guys I had dated—on the panel and in my ward—and wondered whether any of them knew Quick-Draw. He seemed older and more mature than many of them, which seemed like a funny conclusion to draw about a clown who was so great with little kids. I figured Q was probably Barb's age and had simply never married. Maybe he was shy unless he could hide behind a disguise.

I thought about the local guys I knew. Most of them were home from their missions now. James was back from his mission to Italy and was already engaged to a girl from Orange County. Danny and Ron were both back and had gone right up to BYU to get started in summer classes. Maybe I'd see them this fall, I thought.

Just then I noticed that a squad car had pulled over up ahead, its lights twirling. Two policemen were standing with some guy off to the side. I slowed down and looked—were they making an arrest? Oh, my gosh! It was Marky Davis!

As I slowly rolled by, I saw them making him walk a line like they do with drunk drivers. I couldn't believe it! I'd heard he had even served a mission to Hawaii. (See? Lucky Dog Davis would have to go on a mission to the balmiest, most relaxing tropical paradise possible. His luck just slays me.) But much as I'd always known what a baboon he was, I still never thought he'd be a drunk driver! It makes me so furious when Mormons are so careless with their reputations; guys like him make us all look bad. His poor parents, I thought. They'd probably have to bail him out of jail tonight. From valedictorian to town drunk. What a shame.

I almost mentioned it to Q during dinner the next day; we seemed to be sharing so much with each other these days. But the whole subject seemed so depressing I decided not to even bring it up.

"I really admire what you're doing with the children," I said. "You have such a loving way with them. It's really inspiring."

"Inspiring? That's an interesting way to put it. Thank you." His voice was warm and assuring. "I saw you playing the wicked troll today with China."

I blushed. "Oh, you did? Hmm. Well that was her idea," I said. "She's the fair maiden and I'm the antagonist."

"Was that line about repenting her idea? She told you to have the troll repent of his sins?"

I laughed. "Well, no. Actually, I was getting tired of being such a baddy all the time. I thought I might try to slip in a little changed heart."

"But she caught you." Q smiled.

"That's right. She knew that if I had the troll turn over a new leaf, her story was over."

"I heard you say, 'You're right. It was terrible of me to turn your carriage into a hamburger. I think I'll repent and join the good side.'"

Now I was really embarrassed. Here was this wonderful, talented, seemingly very bright guy watching me make a fool of myself in China's role-playing scheme. My face was darkening, but I tried to laugh it off. "Well, what the heck—a troll can only try," I said.

Quick-Draw laughed. "China is so funny. Did you see the look on her face when you announced that you had changed your ways? She was panicked."

My eyes watered as I laughed, thinking of that little girl I love so much. "She's so cute," I said.

Quick-Draw smiled. "She said, 'You can't do that! You're the troll, Louisa!' And then you said, 'Rats! I'm foiled again!'" Quick-Draw looked into my eyes. "If I were a little kid, you would be my favorite friend to play with. You really would."

Suddenly my heart was pounding. "Thank you," I said. Was that *my* voice cracking? What was happening to me? Here I was, eating the worst food on the planet, across from a clown—a *clown*—and I was all full of butterflies or something. I couldn't stop smiling at him. And worst of all, after almost three months of working with him at the hospital, all of a sudden I felt as nervous as though I didn't even know him. I forced my eyes away from his and stared at my salad, trying—uselessly—not to blush. I tore open a packet of salad dressing and poured it over the salad.

And then he touched my hand, which I noticed was shaking. "Louisa, are you nervous?"

My eyes zinged open, but I kept staring at my salad. And then, worse than being a nervous wreck, all at once my eyes started watering and I began sweating. (Perspiring, according to Mom.)

Mom? Mom—wait a minute. In an instant I recalled her standing there in the kitchen, saying, "Louisa, I have a feeling that when *you* fall in love, you'll know it. It'll hit you like a ton of bricks and you won't even remember what you're doing."

Quick-Draw had left his side of the table now and was sitting beside me on the bench, his arm around me. "Louisa, are you all right? You just poured ketchup all over your salad." Suddenly my eyes focused where they'd been staring, and I saw that my salad was covered with red.

"Oh my gosh—oh—I feel so stupid. Um—I'll go get another one." I bolted from the table, everything in a blur, and headed for the pop machine. I stood there for a second until it registered in my brain that this was not the salad bar. I turned, utterly confused, my circuits popping like firecrackers and my poor brain flashing OVERLOAD— OVERLOAD in my head. Frantically, I combed the cafeteria for the salad bar. I dashed over to the hot food counter, and again, stood staring for a minute. This isn't it, I finally deduced. I turned and headed for the ice cream freezer. Once more, I just stared at it like a complete fool. In a few more seconds, I headed toward the pastry counter. I felt like a wind-up car that keeps crashing into the wall, backing up, then crashing again.

The whole room seemed to be charged with electricity. My veins felt as if I'd had a 7-Up transfusion. How can anyone tingle this much and not explode? What on earth was happening to me?

Suddenly Quick-Draw was beside me. "It's okay. I'm here," he whispered. His voice sounded familiar and frightening all at once. His arm felt strong as he led me out of the cafeteria and into a nurse's lounge. Then, gently, he sat me down on a sofa. When I finally dared to look up at him, he was smiling.

"Louisa," he said, and then stopped. "Louisa, I—"

Now I could feel my eyes burning again, as uncontrollable tears spilled down my cheeks. "Q" I said, "I am so embarrassed. I am so sorry. I have no idea what is happening to me. I am so embarrassed."

Now he laughed. "You're starting to repeat yourself." Then he smoothed my hair back. I thought I was going to faint. "Are you all right, Louisa?"

All right? Was he serious? I wanted to run all the way home, lock the door, hide under the bed, and never come out again. I also wanted to throw my arms around him.

"I don't know what happened to me in there," I said. "I've never felt so—well, let's see. It can't be menopause."

Now Q laughed. "Louisa," he said. "Would you go out on a date with me?"

"Yes. I mean yes." Oh, somebody slap my face and help me snap out of this! It was getting ridiculous. And Q was just sitting there, chuckling at me and shaking his head.

"Tomorrow night?"

"Tomorrow. Yes." Huh? Who was this guy—this clown—who had suddenly turned me into a robot? Worse, he now knew that I had no social plans whatsoever. I could barely talk, much less pretend to be busy and try to schedule the date for next week, like I usually do.

My legs felt like jelly.

Q smiled. "I'll pick you up at six, for dinner. Louisa, are you listening to me?" He cupped my face in his hands.

"Uh-huh." My eyelids were both fluttering and my mouth was as dry as Aunt Melva's pot roast. I must have looked like a moth in one of those bug zappers.

Q laughed. "I have to go now, but I'll get your address from personnel. Something tells me this isn't the time to ask you for your house number. Will you be okay?"

"Oh, yes. I'll be fine." In fact, I thought, as soon as you leave, I'll probably come to my senses, buy a one-way ticket to Tanzania, and live in secluded embarrassment forever. I couldn't believe I had fallen apart so completely. What on earth was happening? I managed a weak smile as Q left, and it wasn't until I was driving home that I realized: I didn't even know his name.

That evening I stumbled into the living room, still shaking a little, and collapsed into a chair. My parents were watching TV. At least, I think they were. They were looking in that direction, anyway.

"Louisa, what's wrong with you?" Mom jumped up and felt my forehead. "Look at her, Gordon. She's as white as a ghost. Louisa, what happened?"

Dad turned off the TV—I think—and came over, too. "Louisa?

Can you answer your mother?"

"Look at her, Gordon. Something's wrong with her." Now, instantly hysterical, Mom began shouting, "Louisa, can you hear us? Are you deaf?"

I started giggling. What a ridiculous question—are you deaf—how could anyone ever answer yes to that? It struck me as far funnier than it was, and I began laughing so hard that I cried.

"Look at her, Gordon!" Mother was falling apart. "Louisa, are you on drugs or something? I'm calling Bill to come right over." Now that Bill's a pharmacist, Mom thinks he's the same as any doctor and should be summoned for every medical emergency that happens to arise.

"Now, Janet." Dad's soothing tones. "Pull yourself together, dear."

Mom was cradling my head in her arms now, twisting my neck a little too far, but I was laughing too hard to tell her. Finally I managed a yelp and she let go.

"I'm fine," I said, the laughter subsiding at last. I took a big breath. "Oh, Mom, Dad—I think I'm in love."

Now Mom beamed and Dad frowned. Together they both said, "With whom? You haven't even been dating!"

"That clown at the hospital," I said.

Now Dad frowned even more, having never heard of Q before. "What clown? Who is this clown?"

Mom patted Dad now, suddenly reassuring him just as he had been reassuring her only seconds earlier. "Oh, he's a lovely boy," Mother said. "Louisa's told me all about him. He's quite remarkable."

"So what's his name?" Dad stared at me.

And he kept staring. Suddenly I exploded in laughter again and through my wheezing managed to croak, "I don't know."

"She doesn't know? You're telling me this is a great guy, and she doesn't even know his name?" Dad threw down the TV guide. "Oh, this is just *great.*"

Mom tried to get Dad to sit down now, and simultaneously cast me furious glances. "I'm sure he's a wonderful fellow," she said, and then whipping around to me, "Yes, Louisa—who *is* this clown and why don't you even know his name?"

Now both of them were standing in front of me with their hands on their hips, staring me down and demanding an explanation. And there I was, helplessly weak, head over heels in love, and absolutely unable to do anything but laugh. "You'll meet him tomorrow night," I said. "Then we'll all find out." And I floated off to bed.

The next day passed in stops and starts. Half the time I was so eager to see Q that I could hardly wait until six. And the other half of the time I was a bundle of nerves, wondering what to wear and trying to keep my hands from shaking.

Finally at six, the doorbell rang. I leaped from my chair to answer it.

And there on my porch stood Mark Davis, of all people. What was *he* doing here? What horrible timing; it was six o'clock and Q would probably pull up any minute. The last thing I needed was for Mark Davis to be on the porch and ruin the evening.

"Hi!" Mark said.

"Mark—hello. Long time no see. What are you doing here?" I asked.

Mark laughed. "I'm your date."

"Right. And I'm the Queen of England."

Now Mark grinned. "No, you're the troll. China is the Queen of England."

I gasped. Could this possibly be true? Or was this some cruel joke? Had Mark paid Q to let him come in his place? But then how would he know about China? I was completely astounded. Mark Davis was Q? Impossible!

I smirked. "Okay. Q told you to say that, right?"

Mark began cracking up. "You honestly didn't know it was me? Oh, this is hilarious. I thought you knew all along!" Mom and Dad were inside, waiting to meet the man of my dreams, and here I was, arguing with Mark Davis.

I stepped out onto the porch and whispered, "Listen, you and Q have had your little joke, and it was very funny. But you and I both know that you have absolutely nothing in common with Q. So now you can just go home." Mark was doubled over now, and he stumbled down the stairs to the lawn, where he fell over and began to roll around holding his sides.

Disgusted, I finally went in the house and slammed the door.

"Was that him? What happened?" Dad asked.

I rolled my eyes. "Oh, that wasn't him," I said. "That was just that jerk, Mark Davis, pulling another stupid gag. If Q was in on it, then I guess I really misjudged him."

Mom and Dad exchanged looks of confusion and the doorbell rang again.

Maybe it was Q this time, I thought, and opened the door. Ugh. Mark Davis again. "Mark," I said, as gently as I could, "enough is enough. Please?"

He was wiping tears from his eyes, still shaking with laughter. "Louisa, it's me. I promise."

I pushed his chest, backing him up onto the porch and stepped outside again. "Look, Mark. I'm going to have to be rude in a minute."

"Louisa, you've got to believe me. Couldn't you tell it was me in that clown suit?"

I sighed. Mark Davis was such a relentless joker. "Mark, first of all, I saw you with the policemen the other night."

"What policemen?"

"When they arrested you for drunk driving. And I realize that you're probably drunk now, as well."

Mark roared with laughter. "Louisa, do you know what that was? I was doing my home teaching!"

"Right. You must think I'm an idiot."

"I was!" Mark could hardly keep from laughing to tell the story. "I was assigned this new, inactive guy and I'd never been to his house. So I was driving down his street, and I couldn't read the addresses. So I kept swerving over to the right to kind of get closer, you know? And wouldn't you know a cop was right behind me and thought I was drunk!"

Now I started chuckling. "Well, that is pretty funny, I have to admit."

"No, it gets worse," Mark said. "So the cop gives me this test or whatever it is, and wouldn't you know—it's on the lawn of the very guy I need to home teach! Boy, talk about making a great first impression. It's nearly as bad as that time you saw me wearing a popcorn box hat as I was coming out of the movies."

"You saw me? I can't believe you remember that."

"Are you kidding? I've had a crush on you ever since that youth conference when I had to be a hula dancer. I was so embarrassed that all I could do was laugh. It was horrible!"

Now I smiled. The voice, the style. It was all so familiar. Could he really be Q or was my mind still shot from last night's mental lightning storm?

"So just my luck you had to drive by as I'm being tested for drunk driving. Louisa, I have the weirdest luck in the world."

"I always thought you had incredibly lucky . . . luck. I was always . . . jealous, I guess. It seemed like you got away with murder. You were always goofing off and getting away with it."

Mark shook his head. "No way. I spent my entire childhood in hot water. That's probably why I can't swim to this day."

"You can't swim?"

"No way. So where do I go for my mission? Hawaii, of all places." Now I laughed. "I guess I've really misjudged you, Mark. I hope you'll forgive me. I . . . I thought you were a drunk the other night. Boy, I really went by appearances. I'm sorry."

Mark smiled, and then I saw it. That sweet look in Q's eyes whenever he was about to comfort someone.

"Can I give you a hug?" Mark smiled. "Maybe then you'll believe I'm really Q."

I nodded and he held me. When we pulled apart, both of us had tears in our eyes. "Uh-oh. It's happening again," I said.

"Just like last night," Mark said, running his hands through my hair. "You were so beautiful all messed up like that. You didn't know where you were going. You must have stared at the 7-Up machine for two minutes."

I smiled. "That's because I had 7-Up running through my veins. I haven't felt so scrambled since—hey! Since you spun me around in those teacups."

Mark shook his head. "I was such a wreck, Louisa. I didn't know what to do, what to say—I was so nervous being with you, all I could do was spin that steering wheel."

"It's lucky we both didn't go flying out of there," I said. "You know, when that ride finally stopped, I could hardly walk."

"You? You should have seen me. Or maybe not—I threw up. I don't know if it was the spinning or just being with you, but I was a disaster." We both laughed.

"Hey," I said. "Last night."

"Yeah?"

"When I was so dizzy and you were helping me—your voice sounded so familiar. You said, 'It's okay; I'm here.' That was the same thing you said at the teacup ride. I thought I'd heard it before."

Mark held me in a strong hug, then kissed my forehead. "I've always felt that way about you. Protective or something. I just want to be with you. All the time."

"Why didn't you ever ask me out?"

"Are you kidding? You couldn't stand me!"

I smiled, embarrassed. "You're right. I think I was jealous because you were everything I guess I wanted to be, only I was too . . . proper or chicken or something. You could tell I didn't like you?"

Mark rolled his eyes. "The whole world could tell, Louisa. And I could never understand why. I figured Wendy had told you how tough I was to baby-sit."

"She did, as a matter of fact."

Mark grinned. "It's all true. I was a little brat. But I outgrew it, honest. And when we both started working at the hospital, I figured that you had changed your mind about me."

"Thank goodness for your costume. I might never have given you a chance. I feel so ashamed—"

Mark hugged me again and we kissed. "Louisa," he whispered, "I think you love me."

"What?" I pulled back, and started laughing.

"Well, don't you?"

Now I socked him. "The nerve of some people's children," I said, still laughing. "I think it's supposed to go the other way around, Mark."

He smiled and rubbed his nose against mine. "I know, but . . . you do love me, don't you?"

Now I smiled into the face of my best friend, the man I had grown to love without even knowing his name. It was a face I wanted to look at forever. "Yes," I said. "More than I ever thought possible."

He smiled, and then his eyes started to water. "I love you, too," he said. "I think I always have." He sniffled. "Do you have a Kleenex in your house?"

"Sure, come on in," I said. Mark stepped inside where Mom and Dad were still waiting, and I grabbed a napkin off the kitchen counter and brought it back to him. The tears were really coming now, and I dabbed at his eyes.

"Hey," he said, laughing. "You're getting crumbs in my eye or something."

"Sorry," I said, wiping his tears with my fingers. This was it. This was the one. I knew it down to the tips of my toes, which felt as if they were floating about six inches off the floor. I stared up into his face and said, "Mom and Dad, this is Mark Davis."

And this is your daughter in love.

About the Author

Joni Hilton is the author of numerous novels and nonfiction works specializing in family relationships. She has a Master of Fine Arts degree in professional writing from the University of Southern California, and she writes about parenting and family relationships for several national magazines. She has also been a TV talk show host in Los Angeles, and has instructed parenting classes and worked with inner-city moms to teach them parenting skills.

Joni and her husband, Bob, live with their four children in Sacramento, California. Next to mothering and writing, Joni enjoys creative cooking, and has entered her award-winning recipes in many state and national cook-offs.